PRAISE FOR JERROLD ZIVIC AND HIS WORK

Working with Mr. Zivic over the past 25 yrs has proven to be very rewarding. In my position as a claim representative, one of my responsibilities is to refer disabled employees to a fair and responsive SSD representative. Mr. Zivic proved time and time again his extensive knowledge in the field of SSD. My disabled employees always found him eager to do his very best representation so they would obtain the very best results. Thank-you Mr. Zivic for always giving 110% to your clients! --- Betty A – LTD Benefit Specialist

I would like to take this opportunity to tell you that Mr. Zivic was a superb attorney. He was most helpful, sympathetic and sincere person anyone in my position could have hoped for to represent me. It was indeed a very nerve racking, emotional and trying time. He was simply brilliant in his ability to calm my nerve and fears to handle this case in a most professional manner. To put it simply – he's the greatest. --- Peter R

I would just like to say thank you! So very much for all of your time and effort, that you gave me. Also for all of your diligence and patience. Once again I thank you for all of your courtesy I love you guys a lot and will always remember you. Mr. Zivic thank you! G-d bless you always! --- Patricia H

The authors' intention in writing this book is to help you and your family keep your Social Security Disability Benefits.

Many of you have used legal help in the past when you were trying to get your benefits, but with Continuing Disability Reviews, it's difficult to find an attorney.

Jerrold Zivic (along with his son Aaron) put their 30+ years of knowledge to use helping you keep your Social Security Disability Benefits.

HOW TO KEEP
YOUR SOCIAL SECURITY
DISABILITY BENEFITS:

Tips, Tools and Strategies for Success

Volume 1

By:

Jerrold Zivic, J.D.
&
Aaron Zivic, J.D., M.P.A.

First Electronic Edition: November 2017

First Print Edition: December 2017

eBook & Print Book design & formatting by D. D. Scott's LetLoveGlow Author Services

DISCLAIMER

The information provided in this book will help you preserve your Social Security Disability Benefits. It's provided "as is" without any representations or warranties, express or implied, by either of the authors Jerrold Zivic and Aaron Zivic. The opinions in this book are the opinions of the authors. The authors make no representations or warranties as to the legal information or other information provided in this manual. They do not represent or warrant that the information contained in this book is or will always be up-to-date or accurate.

This manual contains general information about Continuing Disability Reviews (CDRs) conducted by the Social Security Administration (SSA) for individuals who receive Social Security Disability Benefits.

This book is not an alternative to legal advice. If you have any specific questions about legal matters, consult with an attorney or other professional service provider. Purchasing or reading this book does not constitute an attorney-client relationship between the authors and the reader of the book.

None of the views expressed in the book are endorsed by or representative of those of the Social Security Administration.

You agree that the authors are not liable to you or others, in any way or for any damages of any kind or under any theory, arising from the use of this book, or your access to or use of or reliance on the information in or through this volume, including but not limited to, liability or damages under contract or tort theories or any damages caused by viruses contained within electronic files of this book or any linked site, regardless of prior notice to us.

DEDICATION

This book is dedicated to all of the hardworking people we have met over the years who never gave a thought to being sick and finding themselves having to apply for Social Security Disability. We admire the strength they've shown in having to adjust their expectations of what their lives would be and in handling adversity. We hope that in some small way, we will be able to help everyone on Social Security Disability keep their disability benefits.

TABLE OF CONTENTS

INTRODUCTION

There are approximately fifteen million people receiving Social Security Disability Benefits. If you are one of the countless beneficiaries who has had to battle to get your Social Security Benefits, even though, for example, you have a growth in your chest the size of a football, have multiple failed back surgeries, suffer from crippling emotional difficulties or a host of other physical or mental impairments, this book is for you. If you are one of the beneficiaries who was awarded their benefits without too much difficulty, remember the one-time rule…just because you were fortunate when you applied for benefits, doesn't mean you won't have to struggle to keep your benefits. So, this book is a must read for you as well.

We congratulate you if you have just been awarded or are receiving ongoing Social Security Disability Benefits! However, your journey with the Social Security Administration (SSA) is just beginning and probably will never be over. Your disability award is not an automatic lifetime benefit. The day you are awarded benefits is the day you should start your mission to keep your benefits.

By law, the Social Security Administration must periodically review existing recipients' conditions to ensure that they still meet SSA eligibility requirements. You will likely be contacted at some point in your life, and depending on your age, maybe multiple times to have your claim reviewed.

You do not want your hard-earned benefits terminated! For many of you, your benefits are a crucial part of your financial security. Feeding your family, keeping a roof over your heads, clothing and all of life's other necessities can be lost if your benefit is terminated.

If you are one of the many beneficiaries who served in the military, was wounded, awarded a medal and later found out you had a difficult disease to cure, don't expect that Social Security will be sympathetic to your situation. Remember that this same agency probably turned you down two times and made you wait over two years to get a hearing then finally paid your claim. You do not want your family to go through the same uncertainty, emotional pain and hardship that it took to get you your benefits in order to keep your benefits. As the military taught you, always be ready.

Maybe you are the person seeking benefits who went to four hearings only to be turned down four times because Social Security could not understand that the side effects of your medications were preventing you from working. You must immediately prepare to keep your benefits.

Can you survive without your benefits for the five plus years it took you to finally win your case? Remember that feeling of joy at the fifth hearing when you finally won your benefits and how your family's life got better. The impact on your spouse and children of not having the resources to take care of their needs cannot be measured, along with the stress you've coped with which does not help your health.

When you get called to have your case reviewed, be prepared, organized and have a plan.

You should never be apologetic about getting Social Security Disability Benefits or trying to keep them. You have paid for these benefits! When the Government takes out FICA in each person's paycheck, that is how we're paying the premiums for Title II Social Security Disability Benefits. This is not charity. You have worked hard, and if, unfortunately, you get sick, this is a program that is designed to protect you.

The review process is referred to as a Continuing Disability Review (CDR), and applies to both Social Security Disability Insurance (SSDI) as well as Social Security Insurance (SSI) beneficiaries. If the SSA determines that your medical condition has improved to where you can reasonably be expected to resume working, your benefits will end.

This book is designed to prepare you for a CDR. Please remember that the SSA will only send a CDR by mail. Do not be scammed by any email that represents itself to be from the SSA.

With this book, you will be equipped with the information and tools you need in order to keep your benefits. We have provided you with a handy checklist to make it even easier!

For many of you, getting your benefits took years. There was likely financial and emotional stress placed on you and your family – the possible loss of your house, how to pay your bills, how to find medical treatment and more. Getting your benefits is just the beginning. Most of you will need to keep them.

The Facts:

Winning your disability case is a great relief, but SSA can periodically review your disability and eligibility. You need to prepare and be ready!!

We anticipate that Social Security is going to continue to expand its use of CDRs for a variety of reasons. It makes no difference what the reasons are, however. You need to be ready.

A record number of Americans are on government disability rolls. As of May 2013, SSA reported there are 15,000,000 beneficiaries either on SSDI or SSI.[1] It is not surprising then, that considering the current state of the economy, the political climate, the record number of people getting older, along with this record number of disability beneficiaries, the federal government is looking to reduce the amount of spending on disability insurance. One method for decreasing the amount of money distributed to disability recipients is through CDRs.

The SSA has been increasing the number of full medical CDRs performed. The objective of the SSA is to review as many cases as they can to ensure that no person receiving benefits is no longer entitled to these benefits. The most recent statistics reflect that SSA has conducted

---

[1] https://www.ssa.gov/policy/docs/quickfacts/stat_snapshot/

approximately 2,000,000 CDRs in the past fiscal year.[2] This is an exponential increase in the number of reviews over the past four years.

The only thing that seems to slow the SSA down is the lack of funds to process these reviews. The lack of funds also slows down their ability to complete a review once it's started. So, if you are being reviewed, it probably will not be a very quick process. You need to be ready immediately, though, to defend your claim.

Your goal is to make it as easy as possible for the SSA to approve your ongoing benefit. We are going to show you how to do that.

The Facts:

SSA is seeking to expand the number of CDRs performed. Your case could be reevaluated!

One thing to keep in mind is that if you obtained legal representation during your initial disability proceedings, don't assume you can retain a lawyer again for your CDR.

---

[2] https://www.ssa.gov/open/data/Periodic-Continuing-Disability-Reviews.html

During your original case when you were approved for disability, your representative was entitled to receive 25% of your back-benefits (up to $6,000). CDRs, on the other hand, do not provide a way for an attorney or representative to get paid. Legal fees are usually paid out of past due benefits. With CDRs, there almost never is a past due benefit. Attorneys or representatives are reluctant to assist a Claimant without the security of knowing he/she will get compensated for their efforts. Your promise to pay generally will not be enough to hire an attorney or representative.

Remember, too, that all attorney or representative fees must be approved by the SSA. It is a crime for anyone to charge a fee in a Social Security Disability case without prior approval of the Administration. If you are told by an attorney or representative that there is an upfront fee, run far away. They can arrange to have monies held in an escrow account, but the fee still must be approved by the SSA and funds not released until then.

If you are receiving long term disability insurance and the insurance company is taking an offset from the disability money you receive from Social Security, you should contact the insurance company about helping to get you an attorney. The insurance company has a lot of money at stake in you keeping your benefit, so they should be willing to help you pay for one. The insurance company may want to recommend an attorney. You can certainly take the name, but you have every right to hire your own attorney, and the insurance company should still be willing to pay for this attorney. You are not required to take the insurance company's recommendation.

The Facts:

Since it could be difficult to find a lawyer, you must be prepared to go it on your own.

CHAPTER 1

WHAT TO DO BEFORE YOU EVER GET A CDR

The day after you receive your award of disability is the day you need to start to prepare for a review of your case.

By the same token, you need to take care of your health, even if it's not convenient. It's important to see your medical provider on a regular basis. Letting years go by without seeing a health care provider is risky for both your health and being able to keep your Social Security Disability Benefit. It is key for the SSA to see that you have had ongoing medical care. If you were a Judge, for example, and somebody came before you saying they were sick but they never went to see a doctor what would you think?

The very first thing you need to do is purchase an inexpensive spiral notebook…the kind we used to purchase for each class in school. (Yes, there are still paper spiral notebooks.) The spiral notebook can be one of the best investments you ever make.

The reason we suggest a spiral notebook is that it is hard to lose the pages. It always seems that when you use a binder-type notebook, the page you are looking for gets lost. If you use your computer or some other electronic device, be sure to back up regularly.

It is your responsibility to know where and when you have received medical treatment and anything else that you have done to manage your disability. Social Security is not an investigator. And even if you do find someone to represent you, they are not investigators, either. Be responsible for yourself. We can't tell you the number of times we've been told "*they* have the records." We have never been able to figure out who "*they*" are. The only person that knows about your treatments is you!

Later on in the process when you're preparing the long form CDR application, you are going to be more than glad you have your spiral notebook. In the notebook, you are going to keep track of all of your medical appointments, support group appointments, medicines purchased and anything and everything that pertains to your disability.

When you go to the doctor, prepare a list of all of your problems and questions and make sure the doctor addresses each one. You also need to make sure that the medical provider is noting your problems in your medical chart. Do not be bashful about insisting this gets done – the medical provider works for you, and part of good care includes making careful notes.

Note: With electronic record-keeping today, medical providers are spending a lot of the time of your visit with their face in a computer. Make sure that they actually examine you.

Keep Your Benefit Tip:

Record the date you went to the Doctor, the Doctor's name and the reason for the visit.

By receiving regular medical treatment, the SSA can easily recognize that you have ongoing care for your medical problems. A continuing course of treatment goes a long way to proving you have medical problems. Social Security takes the position that if you are not getting treatment(s), there is nothing wrong with you.

Even if there is little a doctor can do for you, you must go at least once a year, list your complaints and issues, and if your condition has not improved, make sure that is noted in the record. You also never know whether or not there's been an advance in medical care for your condition(s), so it's good to touch base with your medical providers.

If you have improved, have the doctor explain in your medical record what the improvement is and why he/she feels that you are still unable to work **any** type of job. Finally, if your condition has gotten worse, have that detailed in the medical record and how that further restricts your ability to work.

The Facts:

Social Security is not concerned if you can do your past work. Their concern is whether or not you are capable of doing any kind of work.

If you have difficulty finding medical care for any number of reasons, you must try to find free care. Note in your notebook every agency you call trying to get care, the date you call and who you speak to, along with the reply. If you can prove that you have made every reasonable effort to get care with your documentation, this will help explain why you have not received care for your problems.

You should also keep track of what self-care options you have tried — maybe yoga, massages, medicinal baths, dietary supplements, etc. If you have read articles, keep copies of those that support what you've done to try to help your condition(s).

Keep Your Benefit Tip:

Go to your physician as often as is medically necessary, but at least once per year. Get a copy of your medical records before you leave the office and have your provider complete one of the medical forms provided in this book.

Go to your physician as often as is medically necessary, but as we have already noted, we cannot stress enough that you go at least once per year. Get a copy of your medical record before you leave the office and have the doctor complete one of the medical forms we provide. The forms are physician-friendly and will not take much time for your medical provider to complete. You are not asking for a narrative just short answers. If the doctor says he/she needs time to prepare the report or provide the medical record – set a date when you can come back to pick them up. Do not rely upon the medical provider to forward what you need. Some offices are great, but you can't gamble on getting your records. If you follow up and do it yourself, you know it will be done.

If you are a gambler and rely upon your records being mailed, the wild card of the U.S. Postal Service is in the mix. Routinely, when we were practicing, our office received misaddressed mail and mail belonging to other people. If we were getting other peoples' mail, no doubt ours also went elsewhere. Be proactive and do not rely upon anybody to do anything for you. If you rely upon yourself, you know it will get done.

Part of good medical care is helping you keep your disability benefits so that you can continue with that care. Your medical provider needs to recognize that he/she has a professional responsibility to help you. Your medical provider also has a financial interest in making sure you remain on disability and have access to the health care insurance that comes with your program. (We have always wondered why many medical providers charge large sums for records when they are the primary beneficiaries of your health insurance.)

Another thing to remember is to keep track of your medications. At least once per year, get a print out from your pharmacy of all of the prescriptions you are taking. This is a great visual for the SSA to see how many medications you are taking. Also, keep copies of the side effects these medications can give you. If you experience any of these side effects, let the SSA know.

CHAPTER 2

WHEN DOES A CDR TYPICALLY HAPPEN?

It would be nice to be able to plan when you will receive a CDR, but this is very difficult. It's like jury duty in many jurisdictions… the notice just shows up and of course it's at the most inconvenient time. So, always be ready to prove that you are still disabled.

When a person is judged disabled, the disability determination specialist employed by the SSA sets a time in the future at which the claim will be reexamined. This is what is referred to as a "diary date," and it indicates a time frame in which the next CDR will be scheduled. The amount of time between CDRs is variable, ranging anywhere from 3 to 7 years You are not notified what your diary date is.

The Facts:

Your claim can be reviewed anywhere from 3-7 years from your onset date or if a triggered event occurs.

The timing can depend upon several factors. The biggest factor is the severity of your impairment(s) and the likelihood of recovery. If your condition is less severe and is expected to improve, you might receive a CDR notice in less than 3 years. On the other end of the spectrum, if your condition is more serious, such as a permanent disability (e.g. lost limb), and your condition is not expected to improve, you might receive notice in 7 years. Age of the individual is also an important factor. Individuals under the age of 50 are likely to undergo CDRs more frequently than individuals over 50. Some beneficiaries nearing retirement age may not receive notice at all.

Many times, however, Social Security ignores all of these commonsense factors. Another factor that comes into play is how much money SSA has allocated for CDRs, and that is always difficult to determine. Congress seems to routinely fail to provide Social Security with enough funds to manage the many different programs it is responsible for.

Basically, you should be prepared to receive a CDR notice at almost any time. Below are five classifications that will influence how frequently SSA will conduct a CDR…

> 1. **Medical Improvement Not Expected (MINE):** Conditions for which recovery is not expected or are permanent. This category may also include a condition, which may not be permanent, but because of the individual's age and skills there is a low likelihood for medical improvement. SSA will review once every 5 to 7 years.
> 2. **Medical Improvement Possible (MIP):** Conditions that are not expected to improve. SSA will review once every 3 years.

3. **Medical Improvement Expected (MIE):** Conditions that improve with time/rest. SSA will review 6 to 18 months following the initial finding of disability.

4. **Vocational Re-examination cases:** SSA will review recipients enrolled in a vocational program.

5. **Miscellaneous Factors:** Advances in technology that allow an individual to return to work or another person reports to the SSA that an individual has returned to work or recovered.

Here's an example of how a Medical Improvement decision is made as it applies to a beneficiary's ability to work:

You were 65 inches tall and 246 pounds at the time your disability was established. You had venous insufficiency and persistent edema in your legs. At the time, your ability to do basic work activities was affected because you were able to sit for 6 hours, but were able to stand or walk only occasionally. At the time of the continuing disability review, you had undergone a vein stripping operation. You now weigh 220 pounds and have intermittent edema. You are still able to sit for 6 hours at a time and to stand or walk only occasionally although you report less discomfort on walking. Medical improvement has occurred because there has been a decrease in the severity of the existing impairment as shown by your weight loss and the improvement in your edema. This medical improvement is not related to your ability to work, however, because your functional capacity to do basic work activities (i.e. the ability to sit, stand and walk) has not increased.

Did You Know That?
When children turn 18, SSA automatically reviews their claim.

CDRs FOR CHILDREN

When children turn 18, those who are currently receiving SSI Disability Benefits will have their claims reviewed. The reason for this automatic review stems from the fact that different standards are used by the SSA to qualify adults and children for disabilities. Therefore, at age 18, the child must be evaluated under the SSA adult standards. In a nutshell, you will have to prove that the child will not be able to do any kind of work, at all. It makes no difference whether or not anyone will hire the child for a job. It is only whether or not they are capable of working in a job.

Note: Newborns who receive SSI owing to a low-birth weight will have their claim reviewed upon their first birthday.[3]

TRIGGERED CDRs

In addition to the above regularly scheduled CDRs, the SSA may conduct a CDR in any of the following situations:

---

[3] http://www.disabilitysecrets.com/resources/social-security-disability/ssdi/keeping-benefits-continuing-reviews.htm

•You return to work
•You successfully complete a trial work period or report substantial earnings
•You inform SSA that your condition has improved
•Your medical evidence indicates that your condition has improved
•A third-party informs SSA that you are not following your treatment regimen or are engaged in substantial gainful activity (SGA)
•A new treatment or advances in technology for your disabling condition has recently been introduced[4]
•An SSI recipient transfers from section 1619b status to regular payments[5] (this generally means you have higher earnings.)

CHECKLIST OF THINGS TO DO

☐ Keep a small notebook of doctor appointments for as long as you are receiving disability benefits.

☐ Obtain a copy of your medical record immediately following every doctor appointment or other medical provider appointment.

☐ Once a year, obtain a printout of your medications from your pharmacy.

---

[4] Id.
[5] http://www.ssa.gov/open/data/Periodic-Continuing-Disability-Reviews.html

☐ Ask your Doctor to complete a Residual Functional Capacity Form at least once every 18 months. (This form is included in this volume.)

☐ If you receive correspondence from SSA, it is important to fill out the forms and comply with all SSA requests.

☐ Make copies of the forms you submit to SSA for your personal records. It will make future CDRs much easier.

☐ If you still have questions, visit SSA.gov or your local field office and try to find local assistance groups such as legal aid.

CHAPTER 3

YOU'VE GOT MAIL…A CDR

So now you know when to expect to receive a CDR. But what exactly will you receive in your mailbox? Below is a sample Notice of a Continuing Disability Review.

Social Security Administration
Retirement, Survivors, and Disability Insurance
Notice of Continuing Disability Review

Office of Disability Operations
1500 Woodlawn Drive
Baltimore, Maryland 21241

DATE:
CLAIM NUMBER:

We must regularly review the cases of people getting disability benefits to make sure they are still disabled under our rules. It is time for us to review your case. This letter explains how we plan to start our review of your case

What You Should Do

Please complete the form enclosed with this letter. Answer all the questions on the form because they are very important. They ask about your health problems and any work you did within the last 2 years.

We have enclosed an envelope for you to use. If there is no envelope with this letter, please send the signed form to us at the address shown above.

If We Do Not Hear From You

You should return the form within 10 days after you receive it. If we do not hear from you in that time, we will contact you again.

If you don't give us the information we need or tell us why you cannot give us the information, we may stop your benefits. Before we stop your benefits, we will send you another letter to tell you what we plan to do.

When We Receive The Completed Form

- If we need more information we will call you. If you do not have a telephone, please give a number where we can leave a message for you.

- The information you give us now will help us decide when we should do a full medical review of your case. We will let you know within 90 days after we receive the completed form whether or not we need to do a full medical review now.

It outlines the following essential information:

☐ That your Disability eligibility is currently being reviewed
☐ The precise reason for the review
☐ The medical improvement standard that applies to your claim
☐ The review may lead to the termination of your benefits
☐ That you are permitted to submit medical records or other evidence

---

Keep Your Benefit Tip:

When you receive a CDR in your mailbox, do not panic. Read it carefully and review the checklist we've provided.

Before we review a CDR in detail, it's important to be aware of the nuts and bolts of how CDRs came about. Below is a summary of the law, history and latest developments.

APPLICABLE LAW

20 C.F.R. § 404.1594
§ 404.1594 How we will determine whether your disability continues or ends.
Effective: August 24, 2012

"There is a statutory requirement that, if you are entitled to disability benefits, your continued entitlement to such benefits must be reviewed periodically. If you are entitled to disability benefits as a disabled worker or as a person disabled since childhood, or, for monthly benefits payable for months after December 1990, as a disabled widow, widower, or surviving divorced spouse, there are a number of factors we consider in deciding whether your disability continues.

> 1)We must determine if there has been any medical improvement in your impairment(s) and, if so, whether this medical improvement is related to your ability to work.
> 2)If your impairment(s) has not medically improved, we must consider whether one or more of the exceptions to medical improvement applies.
> 3)If medical improvement related to your ability to work has not occurred and no exception applies, your benefits will continue."

* Note: We'll expand on this in Volume 2*

The Facts:

The SSA must demonstrate that you are currently able to engage in substantial gainful activity before they can find you are no longer disabled.

BRIEF HISTORY OF CDRs

CDRs have been part of the SSDI and SSI programs for a long time to ensure that the government is not providing income to individuals who have recovered from their injury and are able to resume working. However, the enforcement of CDRs has been inconsistent over the years.

In 1980, the SSA instituted several amendments that resulted in more CDRs. It came as no surprise that the upsurge in CDRs led to an increase in "recovery rates" between 1980 and 1982. (A recovery rate is where an individual is able to do full-time work.) In 1983, political winds and negative public reaction to individuals being stripped of benefits led to a temporary moratorium on CDRs for most mental impairment cases. Due to fewer CDRs, recovery rates again fell below pre-1980 levels.

The Facts:

CDRs are not a new phenomenon. They have been around since the 1980's.

The moratorium essentially remained the status quo for CDRs until 1996 when a Republican-led Congress introduced the Contract with America Advancement Act. This initiative authorized additional funds for CDRs for the years 1996-2002.[6] As a result, the recovery rate increased as the SSA began performing more medical CDRs.

---

[6] 42 U.S.C. § 401(g)(1)(A)

In 2003, the additional funding for CDRs expired. Around that time, the SSA deemphasized CDRs and directed its attention toward processing the growing number of initial disability claims paid. That is, rather than using CDRs to review existing cases, the SSA would enact harsher standards at the outset to reduce the number and/or amount of initial disability benefits rewarded. Consequently, the number of medical CDRs performed by SSA dropped from an all-time high of 876,802 in FY2000 to 207,637 in FY2007, before climbing back up to 443,233 in FY2012.[7]

Did You Know That?

The number of CDRs has been rising steadily in the past few years.

For more statistical figures, go to:
http://www.ssa.gov/OACT/ssir/SSI12/V_D_Redet_CDRda ta.html

---

[7] FY2000 data is from the Social Security Advisory Board, Aspects of Disability Decision Making: Data and Materials, February 2012, Table 13, p. 18, http://www.ssab.gov/Details-Page/ArticleD/217/CHARTBOOK-Aspects-of-disability-Decision-Making-Data-and-Materials-February-2012, while FY2007 and FY2012 data is from the Social Security Administration, Social Security Administration, Performance and Accountability Report, Fiscal Year 2012, November 8, 2012, p. 80, http://www.ssa.gov/finance/.

LATEST DEVELOPMENTS

The Inspector General has recently issued two reports concerning the CDR process. These are available at http://oig.ssa.gov/audits-and-investigations/audit-reports/all. Here's a brief summary of these reports:

The Medical Improvement Review Standard During Continuing Disability Reviews No. A-01-13-23065 (May 2014)

The previous SSA Commissioner requested in 2012 for the Office of the Inspector General (OIG) to "determine how many beneficiaries could be removed from the disability rolls if medical improvement review standard (MIRS) was not in place."
This report, in part, stated:

OBJECTIVE

Our objectives were to (a) determine whether the Social Security Administration (SSA) would consider beneficiaries disabled using the Initial Disability Standard, rather than the Medical Improvement Review Standard (MIRS), during continuing disability reviews (CDR) and (b) evaluate data on the MIRS exceptions.

BACKGROUND

The SSA is required to perform CDRs for individuals receiving disability benefits under Titles II and XVI of the

Social Security Act.[8] In addition, the SSA is required to use MIRS in determining whether disability benefits should continue.[9] Under MIRS, an individual's disability continues unless the (1) disabling condition has improved since the last favorable disability determination or comparison point decision (CPD) and (2) individual can engage in substantial gainful activity (SGA).[10]

Medical improvement is shown as a decrease in the medical severity of the disabling condition that was present when the CPD was made. The determination of a decrease in medical severity must be based on changes—or improvement—in the symptoms, signs, and/or laboratory findings associated with the disabling condition(s).[11] If the SSA determines the individual has medically improved, it must also determine whether the medical improvement is related to his/her ability to work.

The Social Security Act provides exceptions to MIRS.[12] These exceptions allow the SSA to find disability ceased in

---

[8] Generally, the frequency of CDRs is dependent upon SSA's assessment of the likelihood of medical improvement. 20 C.F.R. §§ 404.1590(d) and 416.990(d).

[9] MIRS was established with Pub. L. No. 98-460, 98 Stat. 1794 (1984). See also, Social Security Act §§ 223(f) and 1614(a)(4), 42 U.S.C. §§ 423(f) and 1382c(a)(4). However, MIRS does not apply to Title XVI Age-18 Redetermination cases. See Appendix A for additional information.

[10] SSA determines SGA for Title II and XVI adult cases. 20 C.F.R. §§ 404.1594(f) and 416.994(b)(5). See also SSA, POMS, DI 28005.001 (April 11, 2008), DI 28010.105 (June 12, 2001) and DI 28020.050 (October 1, 1997).

[11] 20 C.F.R. §§ 404.1579, 404.1594, and 416.994; SSA, POMS, DI 28010.015 (April 12, 2010).

[12] Social Security Act §§ 223(f) and 1614(a)(4), 42 U.S.C. §§ 423(f) and 1382c(a)(4).

limited situations without showing medical improvement occurred, but evidence clearly shows the person should no longer be, or never should have been, considered disabled.[13]

There are two groups of exceptions to MIRS for adults. Group I exceptions require a finding that the individual is not currently disabled (that is, a finding of ability to engage in SGA) before any finding under the CDR evaluation process that disability has ended. The Group I exceptions are:

> • vocational therapy (any additional education or training that improves the individual's ability to meet the vocational requirements of more jobs), new or improved diagnostic or evaluative techniques, and
> • substantial evidence demonstrates that any prior disability decision was made in error.

Group II exceptions do not require a medical determination of disability and are fraud or similar fault,[14] failure to

---

[13] Social Security Act §§ 223(f) and 1614(a)(4); 42 U.S.C. §§ 423(f) and 1382c(a)(4); 20 C.F.R. §§ 404.1579, 404.1594, and 416.994; SSA, POMS, DI 28020.001 (October 6, 1997).

[14] Fraud exists when a claimant (or any other person acting on the claimant's behalf) with intent to defraud either makes or causes to be made a false statement or a misrepresentation of a material fact for use in determining rights to Title II or XVI benefits; or conceals or fails to disclose a material fact for use in determining rights to Title II or XVI benefits. Similar fault does not require fraudulent intent. It exists when a claimant or any other person either knowingly makes an incorrect or incomplete statement that is material to the determination or knowingly conceals information that is material to the determination. 20 C.F.R. §§

cooperate or whereabouts unknown,[15] and failure to follow prescribed treatment.[16]

Generally, State Disability Determination Services (DDS) make the initial CDR determination using the SSA's regulations.[17] If an individual disagrees with the initial determination, the SSA's regulations give him/her the right to file an appeal within 60 days from the date of notification of the determination. In most cases, an individual may request up to four levels of appeal: (1) reconsideration by a DDS, (2) hearing by an administrative law judge (ALJ), (3) review by the Appeals Council, and (4) review by a Federal Court.[18]

In September 2012, then-SSA Commissioner Astrue requested that the MIRS process be reviewed to determine how many beneficiaries could be removed from the disability rolls if MIRS were not in place.

404.1594(e)(1) and 416.994(b)(4)(i). See also SSA, POMS, DI 27505.015 (June 5, 2008).

[15] A failure to cooperate or whereabouts unknown issue may arise at any point during a CDR when a disabled individual does not furnish medical or other evidence, fails to attend a consultative examination by a certain date, or cannot be located. 20 C.F.R. §§ 404.1594(e)(2), 404.1594(e)(3), 416.994(b)(4)(ii) and 416.994(b)(4)(iii). See also SSA, POMS, DI 28075.005 (December 28, 2012).

[16] If treatment can restore the ability to work, an individual must follow prescribed treatment to receive benefits. If prescribed treatment is not followed without good cause, SSA should cease benefits when performing a CDR. 20 C.F.R. §§ 404.1594(e)(4) and 416.994(b)(4)(iv). See also SSA, POMS, DI 23010.005 (March 30, 2007).

[17] CDRs are performed by DDSs in each of the 50 States, plus the District of Columbia, Puerto Rico, Guam, the U.S. Virgin Islands, and SSA Federal units including the Offices of Central Operation and International Operations.

[18] 20 C.F.R. §§ 404.900 through 404.985 and 416.1400 through 416.1485.

In April 2013, reviewers obtained a file of all CDRs processed in Calendar Year (CY) 2012. From this file, 196,183 adults were identified with a CDR continuance because of no medical improvement in CY 2012. A random sample of 275 was selected for further review and of that sample, 62 cases were forwarded to the SSA for expert case analysis. The SSA was asked to review the cases using the Initial Disability Standard, rather than MIRS,[19] to determine whether an initial allowance would be granted for disability benefits based on the available evidence.

A separate population of 9,517 adults was also identified in SSA's systems as having a CDR cessation because of a MIRS exception in CY 2012. A random sample from each type of exception was also selected—for a total of 196 cases in review.[20]

---

[19] SSA uses different adjudicative standards for initial disability claims and CDRs. The Agency has a 5-step sequential evaluation process to adjudicate initial disability claims and an 8-step evaluation process for CDRs. 20 C.F.R. §§ 404.1520(a)(4), 404.1594(f), 416.920(a)(4) and 416.994(b)(5). See also SSA, POMS, DI 22001.035 (March 3, 2003) and DI 28005.010 (October 1, 1997).

[20] We only reviewed cases with a CDR completed in CY 2012. SSA expressed concerns that our results may be understated because our population of individuals with full medical CDRs conducted in CY 2012 did not include some individuals who did not have a CDR but may not be disabled if MIRS were not in place. The Agency uses a profiling methodology to identify individuals for CDRs who are most likely to be ceased under current rules and regulations.

RESULTS OF THE REVIEW

The review resulted in an estimation that, after all appeals, the SSA would pay about $269 million in benefits (until the next CDR due date) to about 4,000 adult beneficiaries who would not be disabled if the SSA used the Initial Disability Standard, rather than MIRS, during a CDR.[21] Additionally, although the cessation determinations were correct, the reviewers found issues with the reason coded for the cessation of some types of MIRS exceptions.

Full Medical Continuing Disability Review Cessations Reversed at the Reconsideration Level of Appeal, No. A-07-13-23019 (April 2014):

The Medical Improvement Review Standard During CDRs (A-01-13-23065)

The SSA took a sample of 50 SSDI and SSI beneficiaries whose cessation decisions were reversed at the reconsideration level in 2012. What was found was that when documentary evidence or testimony became available

---

[21] We initially estimated SSA would pay about $573 million in benefits until the next CDR due date to about 8,500 beneficiaries who would no longer be disabled if SSA used the Initial Disability Standard, rather than MIRS, during the initial CDR. We reduced this estimate to reflect the estimated rate of cessations reversed for adults, after all appeals, reported by the Agency. SSA, Annual Report on Continuing Disability Reviews Fiscal Year 2011, September 2013. Furthermore, we did not adjust our estimates to reflect beneficiaries who might leave the disability rolls before the next CDR due date or for future cost of living adjustments in benefits.

at this level that was not presented earlier, a significant number of initial cessations were reversed.

Interestingly, it was found in some cases that benefits were denied even when the file was missing. SSA policy states that when the folder is lost and cannot be reconstructed, benefits are to be continued.

The only recommendation was that the SSA apply the appropriate policy to determine whether to reopen the cases of the "inaccurate" reconsideration reversal of the initial cessation decision. SSA agreed.

The bottom line here is that the SSA is continually searching for ways to make CDRs cost-effective to perform and with rules that can be understood. As you can see from the two reports above, this is not easy to do.

We know that CDRs are a good thing to do, but the method needs to be more transparent and the SSA needs to make sure the public understands that their motivations are pure, not just cost-savings. What SSA has been struggling with, for what seems like forever, is a way to encourage people to get back to work without risking the loss of their disability benefit. It is difficult for a disabled individual to risk their monthly cash benefit and health insurance for the possibility of a job. For many, the risk is too great.

Keep Your Benefit Tip:

Keep up with any changes in the law which could change how Social Security defines what it means to be disabled. Remember that disabled means you are not able to do any kind of work. It makes no difference whether or not somebody will hire you.

Did You Know That?

Changes in political climate impact CDRs.

CHAPTER 4

WHAT DO YOU DO ONCE YOU RECEIVE NOTICE OF A CDR?

By now you know we advocate that you are always prepared to prove that you are disabled and unable to do any type of work.

The rules and policies for CDRs appear logical, however, it has been our experience that the actual application of these is uneven, and sometimes, the SSA does not follow its own rules and procedures.

The best thing you can do for yourself is keep detailed records of all of your medical treatment. It is almost impossible though for most people to remember all of their medical care over a number of years. For example, do not forget your dentist, and if you go to physical therapy, keep track of this or any gym you go to help recover from one of your physical problems or take account of massage therapy. Basically, keep receipts of all visits to any health care provider and get a yearly printout of medications taken.

If you take dietary supplements, it would be a good idea to keep track of those, too. If you go to a support group, keep track of the dates you attend. Include any and all medical and health care treatment.

Oftentimes, individuals are embarrassed by some type of treatment they are receiving, but this treatment needs to be included. If you are trying some out-of-the-box type of care, that is fine, especially if traditional medical providers have told you there is little they can do to help you. So, don't be uncomfortable about sharing, for example, any type of mental health treatment you may have had or are having. An emotional problem is just as debilitating as a physical problem and many times more difficult to diagnose and treat.

The Facts:

Dental care, Physical Therapy, Massage Therapy and attendance at support groups are all evidence of medical treatment.

As shown in the sample notice letter at the beginning of the previous chapter, the SSA will notify you via United States mail of your impending CDR. They will send you one of two forms:

1.Short-form Disability Update Report (SSA-455-OCR-SM), or the
2.Long-form, Continuing Disability Review Report (SSA-454-BK)

Note: Social Security CDRs often use initials or words that are difficult to understand. Do not worry. We have provided a glossary at the end of this book that you will find most useful.

SHORT-FORM DISABILITY UPDATE REPORT (SSA-455-OCR-SM Scannable Mailer Form & SSA-455 Hard Paper Mailer Form)

Social Security Administration
Disability Update Report
Information and Completion Instructions

Why We Are Writing To You Now	The Social Security Administration must regularly review the cases of people getting disability benefits to make sure they are still disabled under our rules. It is time for us to review this case. Enclosed is a **Disability Update Report** for you to answer to update us about you (or the person for whom you are the representative payee), your health and medical conditions, any recent work activity, or any recent training.
What To Do First	**Please read** the following information, **and** the instructions for completing the report form, **before** you answer the questions.
When to Respond	Please complete the report, **sign it** and send it to us in the enclosed envelope within **30 days**. If there is no return envelope with the report, please send the signed report to us at:
	Social Security Administration P.O. Box 4550 Wilkes-Barre, PA 18767-4550
What We Do With Your Answers	We consider the information you give us together with the information in your claim record to decide if we need to do a full medical review. After we receive the completed report, we will notify you whether or not we need to do a full medical review.
If You Need Help To Answer The Report	It is important that information you give us is accurate. We have tried to make report questions easy to understand and answer. But, if you find that you do not understand a question or questions, please contact us, your authorized representative, a social service agency, your doctor or clinic, or some other person you trust.
If You Need To Contact Us	If you need to contact us, please call us toll-free at **1-800-772-1213** or TTY for the hearing impaired at **1-800-325-0778**. We can answer most questions over the telephone. If you prefer to visit or call one of our offices, please use the 800 number to get the local office address and telephone number. Please have the Disability Update Report with you if you call or visit an office. It will help us answer your questions. Also, if you plan to visit an office, you should call ahead to make an appointment. This will help us serve you.
We May Need To Contact You	Sometimes, we may need more information from you. If so, we will try to call you. If you do not have a telephone, please give us a number where we can leave a message for you. Please print the telephone number in the section provided on the back of the report form.
If We Don't Hear From You	If you do not complete and return the report promptly, or tell us why you cannot respond, we may stop sending payments to you. If it is necessary to stop your payments, we will send you another letter telling you what we plan to do.

If We Do A Full Medical Review	If we decide to do a full medical review of your case, you can give us any information which you believe shows that you are still disabled such as medical reports and letters from your doctors about your health. Then, we look at all your information in your case, including the new information you give us, and decide whether you continue to be disabled under our rules.
Appeals And Continued Benefits	When we review your case, we may find that you are no longer disabled under our rules, and your payments may stop. If your payments stop, you can appeal our decision or you can ask us to continue to make payments while you appeal.
If You Want To Work	Do you want to work, but worry about losing your payments or Medicare before you can support yourself? We want to help you go to work when you are ready. But, work and earnings **may** affect your benefits. Your local Social Security office can tell you more about work incentives, and how work and earnings can affect your benefits.
The Privacy And Paperwork Reduction Acts	**Collection and Use of Personal Information** – Sections 205 and 1631(a)(1) and (b) of the Social Security Act, as amended, and Social Security regulations (20 CFR 404.1589 and 404.1590) authorize us to collect this information. We will use the information you provide to further document your claim and to determine if you are still disabled.

The information you furnish on this report is voluntary. However, failure to provide us with the requested information may prevent us from making an accurate and timely decision on your claim.

We rarely use the information you supply for any purpose other than for reviewing your claim for Social Security benefits. However, we may use it for the administration and integrity of Social Security programs. We may also disclose information to another person or to another agency in accordance with approved routine uses, which include but are not limited to the following:

  1. To enable a third party or an agency to assist Social Security in establishing rights to Social Security benefits and/or coverage;

  2. To comply with Federal laws requiring the release of information from Social Security records (e.g., to the Government Accountability Office and Department of Veterans Affairs);

  3. To make determinations for eligibility in similar health and income maintenance programs at the Federal, State, and local level; and,

  4. To facilitate statistical research, audit, or investigative activities necessary to assure the integrity and improvement of Social Security programs.

We may also use the information you provide in computer matching programs. Matching programs compare our records with records kept by other Federal, State, or local government agencies. Information from these matching programs can be used to establish or verify a person's eligibility for Federally-funded or administered benefit programs and for repayment of loans or delinquent debts under these programs.

A complete list of routine uses for this information is available in our Systems of Records Notices entitled, Claims Files System and the Genesis, the Master Beneficiary Record (00306). These notices, additional information regarding this form, and information regarding our programs and systems are available on-line at www.socialsecurity.gov or at your local Social Security office.

Paperwork Reduction Act Statement – This information collection meets the requirements of 44 U.S.C. § 3507, as required by the Paperwork Reduction Act of 1995. You do not need to answer these questions unless we display a valid Office of Management and Budget (OMB) control number. The OMB control number for this collection is 0960-0511. We estimate that it will take about 20 minutes to read the instructions, gather the facts, and answer the questions. *Send only comments relating to our time estimate above to: SSA, 6401 Security Blvd, Baltimore, MD 21235-6401.* |

~ 37 ~

GENERAL INSTRUCTIONS - HOW TO COMPLETE "SCANNABLE" FORMS	The Disability Update Report is a scannable form which can be "read" electronically. To help us process your report, **please follow these instructions when you answer the questions on the report form:** 1. **USE BLACK INK OR A #2 PENCIL.** 2. **KEEP YOUR NUMBERS, LETTERS, AND "X'S" INSIDE THE BOXES.** 3. **NUMBERS:** Try to make your numbers look like these:

$$0 \quad 1 \quad 2 \quad 3 \quad 4 \quad 5 \quad 6 \quad 7 \quad 8 \quad 9$$

4. **LETTERS:** Print in CAPITALS. Try to make your letters look like these:

$$A \quad B \quad C \quad D \quad E \quad F \quad G \quad H \quad I \quad J \quad K \quad L \quad M$$
$$N \quad O \quad P \quad Q \quad R \quad S \quad T \quad U \quad V \quad W \quad X \quad Y \quad Z$$

5. **MONEY AMOUNTS:** Show dollars only. Do not use dollar signs ($), and do not show cents. For example, show $1,540.30 like this:

Dollars Only, No Cents

$$0 \ 1 \ 5 \ 4 \ 0$$

6. **DATES:** Put a number in each box. For example, show September 9, 2003, like this:

Month   Year

$$0 \ 9 \quad 0 \ 3$$

7. **THE REPORT PERIOD:** The "report period" is the period of time for which we need information. It is described at the top of the report form to the right of your name, and again in questions 1 through 6. Usually, the report period is the last 24 months, but it may be less. **It is important that you keep the report period in mind when answering the questions.**

HOW TO FILL OUT THE REPORT FORM

QUESTION 1.a. - Have You Worked?	If you have not worked during the report period, place an "X" in the box below "NO", and go on to question 2. If you have worked, mark the box below "YES", and answer question 1.b.
QUESTION 1.b. - When You Worked And Your Monthly Earnings	**Describe your most recent work activity first.** Print the months and years you began and ended working in the boxes under "Work Began" and "Work Ended." **If you are working now**, print the current month and year in the first set of boxes under "Work Ended." Print your gross monthly earnings for the periods you worked in the boxes.
QUESTION 2 - School Or Work Training	Place an "X" in the box below "YES" if you have attended school and/or a training program during the report period; otherwise, mark the box below "NO." This could include high school equivalency programs, college courses, vocational evaluation or retraining programs, but generally would not include group therapy or hobbies.

QUESTION 3 - Can You Work?	Tell us if you have discussed with your doctor whether you can return to any kind of work, and if so, whether the doctor told you that you can return to work, even if the work permitted is less physically demanding and/or less stressful than your usual work. **Place an "X" in only 1 box.**
QUESTION 4 - How Is Your Health?	We want to know how your overall health now compares to what it was at the beginning of the report period. You may feel that your health has gotten worse, has improved, or you may feel that your health is about the same and has not gotten better or worse. **Place an "X" in only 1 box.**
QUESTION 5 - Treatment By A Doctor Or Clinic	A "doctor or clinic" can include treatment such as evaluations, checkups, counseling, providing prescriptions or medicine by a doctor, visiting nurse, family health center, psychologist, licensed counseling service, physical therapist, a chiropractor or other licensed health provider. Treatment may be provided in person or by telephone or other contact.
How To Answer Question 5.a.	If you have not been treated by a doctor or clinic during the report period, place an "X" in the box below "NO" and go on to question 6. If you have gone to a doctor or clinic during the report period, mark the box below "YES", and answer question 5.b.
Question 5.b. - Reason For The Visit	**Please start with the most recent visit and then work backwards in time.** Print as much information as will fit, but keep a space between each word. Try to use the most important or key word(s), such as ARTHRITIS or BAD BACK, or HYPERTENSION or HIGH BLOOD. Your medical bills or doctor can provide a short, accurate description.
Date of Visit	Print the month and year you were treated. Complete all 4 boxes. For example, print September 10, 2003, as **09 03**

NOTE: If needed, use the "REMARKS" section on side 2 of the form.

QUESTION 6.a - Have You Been Hospitalized Or Had Surgery?	Place an "X" in the box below "NO" if you have not been hospitalized or not had surgery during the report period. If you have been hospitalized or had surgery during the report period, then place an "X" in the box below "YES" and answer question 6.b.
Question 6.b. - Reason For Treatment	**Please report your most recent treatment first and then work backwards in time.** Try to provide the most important information. Keep a space between each word. Your medical bills or doctor can provide short, accurate words.
Date of Treatment	Print the month and year you were hospitalized or had surgery. Be sure to use all four spaces. **If you were hospitalized more than one month,** print last month you were hospitalized.

NOTE: If needed, use the "REMARKS" section on side 2 of the form.

Remarks Section	If you need more room to answer questions 4.b., 5.b. and/or 6.b., or there are any other facts or statements you want us to consider, place an "X" in the box and write in this section. If necessary, use an extra piece of paper.
Signature, Date and Telephone Sections	Please sign the report form as you usually sign your name. Please provide a telephone number where you can be reached during the day.

Disability Update Report *

DATE:

Social Security Administration, P.O. Box ___, Wilkes-Barre, PA 18767.

FORM APPROVED
OMB NO. 0960-0511

PAYEE'S NAME AND ADDRESS	REPORT PERIOD	
	From	To The Present
	BENEFICIARY	
	TELEPHONE NUMBER	CLAIM NUMBER

Please be sure to **use black ink or a #2 pencil to print your answers.** Also, **read the enclosed instructions** before completing the form. Finally, remember that when answering the questions, **the "REPORT PERIOD" for which we need information about you is from ___ to the present.** If you have any questions, call 1-800-772-1213 or TTY for the hearing impaired at 1-800-325-0778.

1. a. Since ___ have you worked for someone or been self-employed? ⟶   YES ☐   No ☐

b. If you answered "YES" to 1.a., please complete the information below.

	WORK BEGAN		WORK ENDED		MONTHLY EARNINGS
	Month	Year	Month	Year	Dollars Only, No Cents
Most Recent Work 1.	☐☐	☐☐	☐☐	☐☐	$ ☐☐☐☐
2.	☐☐	☐☐	☐☐	☐☐	$ ☐☐☐☐
3.	☐☐	☐☐	☐☐	☐☐	$ ☐☐☐☐

2. Have you attended any school or work training program(s) since ___ ?   YES ☐   No ☐

3. Since ___ to the present...(*Please place an 'X' in one box only*):

☐ my doctor and I have not discussed whether I can work

☐ my doctor told me I cannot work

☐ my doctor told me I can work

4. Place an 'X' in only one box which best describes your health now as compared to ___

☐ BETTER   ☐ SAME   ☐ WORSE

Form SSA-455-OCR-SM (10-02-13)

Continued on the Reverse ⟶

~ 40 ~

5. a. Have you gone to a doctor or clinic for treatment (including evaluations, checkups, counseling, prescriptions, or medicine) since _____?

   b. If you answered "YES" to 5 a., please list:

   YES ☐   NO ☐

Most Recent Visit																					Month		Year	
1.																								
2.																								
3.																								

6. a. Have you been hospitalized or had surgery since _____?

   b. If you answered "YES" to 6 a., please list:

   YES ☐   NO ☐

Most Recent	Reason For (hospitalization or Surgery)																					Month		Year	
1.																									
2.																									
3.																									

REMARKS: If you use this space to further answer questions 1 through 6 place an "X" in the box to the right and print on the lines below. ☐

_____
_____
_____

I declare under penalty of perjury that I have examined all the information on this form, and on any accompanying statements or forms, and it is true and correct to the best of my knowledge. I understand that anyone who knowingly gives a false or misleading statement about a material fact in this information, or causes someone else to do so, commits a crime and may be sent to prison, or may face other penalties, or both.

SIGN HERE ➤	TODAY'S DATE
	TELEPHONE NUMBER (include Area Code)

The short form is a fairly-straightforward, two-page document. The report wants to know what medical treatments you have had during the previous two years. It is typically sent to those beneficiaries whose condition is not expected to improve. A computer subsequently reads the information you submit on the form under a system known as Optical Character Reader (OCR). The form only reaches a human being if the computer determines, based on what's entered on the form by the beneficiary, that he or she may no longer be disabled.

When you receive this notice, the notes and records you have been keeping since you became disabled will come in handy. Everything you need will be at your fingertips, in your spiral notebook.

The only difference between the scannable form and the hard paper form is the question "Would you be interested in receiving rehabilitation or other services that can get you back to work?" Tricky question, isn't it? If you are not able to work at all, why would you have an interest in going back to work? However, a lot of individuals would like to try to work, if they are able to find a way to do so.

Claimants don't want to look like slackers but worry that by answering "yes" it means they're saying they're able to work. Always be honest with the SSA, but be careful not to overstate your abilities. You really don't know for sure that you will be able to return to work, unless you give it a try. So, if you want to go to rehabilitation, you can say "yes." But, that said, it might be a good idea to say you will try but you are not sure if you will be able to complete the rehabilitation or other services offered. Nobody knows for sure until they actually complete the rehabilitation or service.

It also might be a good idea to discuss this with your doctor. Does he or she feel that any of these programs might be detrimental to your health? What are the risks to you if you give it a try?

One way to ensure that your form doesn't get sorted into the pile for further human review is to:

Fill out your information according to the instructions listed below.

Keep Your Benefit Tip:

Print and make sure your writing is legible. You want to make it as easy as possible for SSA to read.

The objective of this form is to simply confirm the information the SSA already has on file. You always want to be honest, but if you do note any positive changes, you might be at risk of losing your benefits. New information will often cause the form to be sent to the stack set aside for further processing or human review. If it is at all possible, you want to defend the original diagnosis for which you were originally awarded disability.

If the form does not get transferred for human review, you will continue receiving your benefits. If your claim does get transferred to a person for additional review, as long as you have been keeping up with your medical treatments and getting the medical evidence and evaluation forms to back up the premise that you are not able to do any kind of work, there is a good chance you will also retain your benefits.

The Facts:

The goal of the CDR is to maintain the status quo and to convey that your disability still prevents you from doing any kind of work.

LONG-FORM CONTINUING DISABILITY REVIEW REPORT (SSA-454-BK)

If your condition is likely to improve or if your answers on the short form signal a warning to the SSA, the agency will send you the long form.

CONTINUING DISABILITY REVIEW REPORT
SSA-454-BK

PLEASE READ THIS INFORMATION BEFORE COMPLETING THIS REPORT

The office that reviews your medical condition will use the information in this report. The information will help that office decide whether you are still disabled. Please complete as much of the report as you can.

IF YOU NEED HELP

You can get help from other people, such as a friend or family member. Please do not ask your health care provider to complete this report. If you cannot complete the report, a Social Security Representative will assist you. If you have an appointment, please have the completed report ready when we contact you.

Note: If you are assisting someone else with this report, please answer the questions as if that person were completing the report.

HOW TO COMPLETE THIS REPORT

- Print or write clearly.
- Include a ZIP or postal code with each address.
- Provide complete phone numbers, including area code. If a phone number is outside the United States, provide International Direct Dialing (IDD) code and country code
- If you cannot remember the names and addresses of your health care providers, you may be able to get that information from the telephone book, Internet, medical bills, prescriptions, or prescription medicine containers.
- ANSWER EVERY QUESTION, unless the report indicates otherwise. If you do not know an answer, or the answer is "none" or "does not apply," please write: "don't know," or "none." or "does not apply."
- Be sure to explain an answer if the question asks for an explanation or if you want to give additional information.
- If you need more space to answer any question, please use Section 11 - Remarks, on the last page to finish your answer. Write the number of the question you are answering.

YOUR MEDICAL RECORDS

If you have any of your medical records covering the last 12 months, send or bring them to our office with this completed report. Please tell us if you want to keep your records so we can return them to you. If you have a scheduled appointment for an interview, bring your medical records, your prescription medicine containers (if available), and the completed report with you.

YOU DO NOT NEED TO ASK DOCTORS OR HOSPITALS FOR ANY MEDICAL RECORDS THAT YOU DO NOT ALREADY HAVE. With your permission, we will request your records. The information that you give us on this report tells us where to request your medical and other records.

Form SSA-454-BK (07-2010) ef (07-2010) Destroy prior editions

The Privacy Act

Sections 205(a), 223(d), and 1631(e) (1) of the Social Security Act, as amended, authorize us to collect this information. The information you provide will be used to make a decision on the named claimant's claim. While giving us the information on this report is voluntary, failure to provide all or part of the requested information could prevent an accurate or timely decision on the named claimant's claim. We generally use the information you supply for the purpose of making decisions regarding claims. However, we may use it for the administration and integrity of Social Security programs. We may also disclose information to another person or to another agency in accordance with approved routine uses, which include but are not limited to the following: (1) to enable a third party or agency to assist Social Security in establishing rights to Social Security benefits and/or coverage; (2) to comply with Federal Laws requiring the release of information about Social Security records (e.g., to the Government Accountability Office and the Department of Veterans Affairs); (3) to make determinations for eligibility in similar health and income maintenance programs at the Federal, State, and local level; and, (4) to facilitate statistical research, audit, or investigative activities necessary to assure the integrity of Social Security programs.

We may also use the information you provide in computer matching programs. Matching programs compare our records with records kept by other Federal, State, or local government agencies. Information from these matching programs can be used to establish or verify a person's eligibility for Federally-funded or administered benefit programs and for repayment of payments or delinquent debts under these programs.

Additional information regarding this form, routine uses of information, and our programs and systems, is available on-line at www.socialsecurity.gov or at any local Social Security office.

The Paperwork Reduction Act

This information collection meets the requirements of 44 U.S.C. § 3507, as amended by section 2 of the Paperwork Reduction Act of 1995. You do not need to answer these questions unless we display a valid Office of Management and Budget control number. We estimate that it will take about 60 minutes to read the instructions, gather the facts, and answer the questions. You may send comments on our time estimate above to: SSA, 6401 Security Boulevard, Baltimore, MD 21235-6401. **Send only comments relating to our time estimate to this address, not the completed report.**

SEND OR BRING THE COMPLETED REPORT TO YOUR LOCAL SOCIAL SECURITY OFFICE, THE NEAREST U.S EMBASSY OR CONSULATE OFFICE. Office addresses are listed under U.S. Government agencies in your telephone directory or you may call 1-800-772-1213 (TTY 1-800-325-0778) for the address.

AFTER COMPLETING THIS FORM, REMOVE THIS SHEET AND KEEP IT FOR YOUR RECORDS.

Form **SSA-454-BK** (07-2010) ef (07-2010)

Form Approved
OMB No. 0960-0072

CONTINUING DISABILITY REVIEW REPORT

For SSA Use Only - Do not write in this box   Date of your last medical disability decision:

Claim Number: _____   Number Holder: _____

Type(s) of Case(s) (Check all that apply)	TITLE II	☐ DIB	☐ DWB	☐ CDB	☐ FZ	☐ ESRD	☐ HB
	TITLE XVI	☐ DI	☐ DIS	☐ DC	☐ BI	☐ BS	☐ BC

If you are filling out this report for the disabled person, please provide information about him or her. When a question refers to "you", "your", or the "disabled person", it refers to the person receiving disability benefits.

SECTION 1- INFORMATION ABOUT THE DISABLED PERSON

1.A. NAME (first, middle initial, last)

1.B. SOCIAL SECURITY NUMBER

1.C. MAILING ADDRESS (Street or PO Box) Include apartment number if applicable

CITY	STATE/Province	ZIP/Postal Code	COUNTRY (if not USA)

1.D. DAYTIME PHONE NUMBER including area code, and the IDD and country codes if you live outside the USA or Canada.

Phone number _____

☐ Check this box if you have a phone or a number where we can leave a message

1.E. Alternate Phone Number, including area code where we may reach you, if any

Alternate phone number _____

1.F. Can you speak and understand English?   ☐ YES   ☐ NO

If no, what language do you prefer? _____
If you cannot speak and understand English, we will provide an interpreter, free of charge.

1.G. Have you used any other names on your medical or educational records in the last 12 months? Examples are maiden name, other married names, or nickname.   ☐ YES   ☐ NO

If yes, please list them here _____

SECTION 2 - CONTACTS

Give the name of a friend or relative (other than your doctors) we can contact who knows about your medical conditions and can help you with your case.

2.A. NAME (first, middle initial, last)

2.B. Relationship to Disabled Person

2.C. MAILING ADDRESS (Street or PO Box) Include apartment number if applicable

CITY	STATE/Province	ZIP/Postal Code	COUNTRY (if not USA)

2.D. DAYTIME PHONE NUMBER (as described in 1.D. above)

_____

2.E. Can this person speak and understand English?   ☐ YES   ☐ NO
If no, what language is preferred? _____

~ 47 ~

SECTION 2 - CONTACTS (continued)

2.F. Who is completing this report?

- ☐ The disabled person listed in 1.A   (Go to **Section 3 - Medical Conditions**)
- ☐ The person listed in 2.A   (Go to **Section 3 - Medical Conditions**)
- ☐ Someone else (Complete the rest of Section 2 below)

2.G. NAME (first, middle initial, last)	2.H. Relationship to Disabled Person

2.I. DAYTIME PHONE NUMBER (as described in 1.D. above)

2.J. MAILING ADDRESS (Street or PO Box) Include apartment number if applicable

CITY	STATE/Province	ZIP/Postal Code	COUNTRY (if not USA)

SECTION 3 - MEDICAL CONDITION(S)

3.A. If you are an adult (age 18 or older), list the physical and/or mental condition(s) (including emotional or learning problems) that limit your ability to work. **If you are completing this report for a child (under age 18)**, list the physical and/or mental condition(s) (including emotional and learning problems) that limit the child's ability to do the same things as other children the same age. **List each physical and/or mental condition separately.**

1
2
3
4

If you need more space go to Section 11 - Remarks on last page

3.B. What is your height without shoes?   OR

feet   inches   centimeters (if outside USA)

3.C. What is your weight without shoes?   OR

pounds   kilograms (if outside USA)

SECTION 4 - WORK
Complete only if you are age 14 years old or older

4. Since the date of your last medical disability decision have you worked? (see date at top of Page 1)

☐ YES (If yes, we may contact you for additional information)   ☐ NO

SECTION 5 - MEDICAL TREATMENT

Within the last 12 months, have you seen a doctor or other health care professional or received treatment at a hospital or clinic, or **do you have a future appointment scheduled:**

5.A. For any **physical** conditions?

☐ YES   ☐ NO

5.B. For any **mental** condition(s) (including emotional or learning problems)

☐ YES   ☐ NO

If you answered "No" to both 5.A. and 5.B., go to Section 6 - Other Medical Information on page 8

Form **SSA-454-BK** (07-2010) ef (07-2010)   PAGE 2

~ 48 ~

SECTION 5 - MEDICAL TREATMENT (continued)

5.C. Tell us who may have medical records covering **the last 12 months** about any of your physical or mental conditions(s) **(including emotional or learning problems)** This includes doctors' offices, hospitals (including emergency room visits), clinics, and other health care facilities. Tell us about your next appointment, if you have one scheduled.

Name of facility or office	Name of health care professional that treated you

ALL OF THE QUESTIONS ON THIS PAGE REFER TO THE HEALTH CARE PROFESSIONAL ABOVE.

PHONE ( ) -	PATIENT ID# (if known)

MAILING ADDRESS

CITY	STATE/Province	ZIP/Postal Code	COUNTRY (if not USA)

Dates of Treatment (within the last 12 months)

1. Office, Clinic or Outpatient visits	2. Emergency Room Visits List the most recent date first	3. Overnight Hospitals Stays
First Visit _____	A _____	A. Date in _____ Date out _____
Last Visit _____	B _____	B. Date in _____ Date out _____
Next Scheduled Appointment (if any) _____	C _____	C. Date in _____ Date out _____

What medical conditions were treated or evaluated?

What treatment did you receive for the above conditions? (Do not describe medicines or tests in the box.)

Check the boxes below for any tests this provider performed or sent you to **within the last 12 months**, or has scheduled you to take. Please give the dates for past and future tests. If you need to list more tests, use **Section 11 - Remarks** on the last page.

☐ Check this box if no tests by this provider or at this facility.

KIND OF TEST	DATES OF TESTs	KIND OF TEST	DATES OF TESTs
☐ EKG (heart test)		☐ EEG (brain wave test)	
☐ Treadmill (exercise test)		☐ HIV Test	
☐ Cardiac Catheterization		☐ Blood Test (not HIV)	
☐ Biopsy (list body part)		☐ X-Ray (list body part)	
☐ Hearing Test		☐ MRI/CT Scan (list body part)	
☐ Speech/Language Test			
☐ Vision Test		☐ Other (please describe)	
☐ Breathing Test			

If you do not have any more doctors or hospitals to describe, go to Section 6 on page 8.

~ 49 ~

SECTION 5 - MEDICAL TREATMENT (continued)

5.D. Tell us who may have medical records covering **the last 12 months** about any of your physical or mental condition(s) **(including emotional or learning problems)**. This includes doctors' offices, hospitals (including emergency room visits), clinics, and other health care facilities. Tell us about your next appointment, if you have one scheduled.

Name of facility or office	Name of health care professional that treated you

ALL OF THE QUESTIONS ON THIS PAGE REFER TO THE HEALTH CARE PROFESSIONAL ABOVE.

PHONE ( ) -	PATIENT ID# (if known)

MAILING ADDRESS

CITY	STATE/Province	ZIP/Postal Code	COUNTRY (if not USA)

Dates of Treatment (within the last 12 months)

1. Office, Clinic or Outpatient visits	2. Emergency Room Visits List the most recent date first	3. Overnight Hospitals Stays
First Visit _____	A. _____	A. Date in _____ Date out _____
Last Visit _____	B. _____	B. Date in _____ Date out _____
Next Scheduled Appointment (if any) _____	C. _____	C. Date in _____ Date out _____

What medical conditions were treated or evaluated?

What treatment did you receive for the above conditions? (Do not describe medicines or tests in the box.)

Check the boxes below for any tests this provider performed or sent you to within the last 12 months, or has scheduled you to take. Please give the dates for past and future tests. If you need to list more tests, use **Section 11 - Remarks** on the last page.

☐ Check this box if no tests by this provider or at this facility.

KIND OF TEST	DATES OF TESTs	KIND OF TEST	DATES OF TESTs
☐ EKG (heart test)		☐ EEG (brain wave test)	
☐ Treadmill (exercise test)		☐ HIV Test	
☐ Cardiac Catheterization		☐ Blood Test (not HIV)	
☐ Biopsy (list body part)		☐ X-Ray (list body part)	
☐ Hearing Test		☐ MRI/CT Scan (list body part)	
☐ Speech/Language Test			
☐ Vision Test		☐ Other (please describe)	
☐ Breathing Test			

If you do not have any more doctors or hospitals to describe, go to Section 6 on page 8.

~ 50 ~

SECTION 5 - MEDICAL TREATMENT (continued)

5.E. Tell us who may have medical records covering **the last 12 months** about any of your physical or mental conditions(s) **(including emotional or learning problems)** This includes doctors' offices, hospitals (including emergency room visits), clinics, and other health care facilities. Tell us about your next appointment, if you have one scheduled.

Name of facility or office	Name of health care professional that treated you

ALL OF THE QUESTIONS ON THIS PAGE REFER TO THE HEALTH CARE PROFESSIONAL ABOVE.

PHONE ( ) -	PATIENT ID# (if known)

MAILING ADDRESS

CITY	STATE/Province	ZIP/Postal Code	COUNTRY (if not USA)

Dates of Treatment (within the last 12 months)

1. Office, Clinic or Outpatient visits	2. Emergency Room Visits (List the most recent date first)	3. Overnight Hospitals Stays
First Visit _____	A _____	A. Date in _____ Date out _____
Last Visit _____	B _____	B. Date in _____ Date out _____
Next Scheduled Appointment (if any) _____	C _____	C. Date in _____ Date out _____

What medical conditions were treated or evaluated?

What treatment did you receive for the above conditions? (Do not describe medicines or tests in the box.)

Check the boxes below for any tests this provider performed or sent you to within the last 12 months, or has scheduled you to take. Please give the dates for past and future tests. If you need to list more tests, use **Section 11 - Remarks** on the last page.

☐ Check this box if no tests by this provider or at this facility.

KIND OF TEST	DATES OF TESTs	KIND OF TEST	DATES OF TESTs
☐ EKG (heart test)		☐ EEG (brain wave test)	
☐ Treadmill (exercise test)		☐ HIV Test	
☐ Cardiac Catheterization		☐ Blood Test (not HIV)	
☐ Biopsy (list body part)		☐ X-Ray (list body part)	
☐ Hearing Test		☐ MRI/CT Scan (list body part)	
☐ Speech/Language Test			
☐ Vision Test		☐ Other (please describe)	
☐ Breathing Test			

If you do not have any more doctors or hospitals to describe, go to Section 6 on page 8.

Form **SSA-454-BK** (07-2010) ef (07-2010)

SECTION 5 - MEDICAL TREATMENT (continued)

5.F. Tell us who may have medical records covering **the last 12 months** about any of your physical or mental condition(s) **(including emotional or learning problems)**. This includes doctors' offices, hospitals (including emergency room visits), clinics, and other health care facilities. Tell us about your next appointment, if you have one scheduled.

Name of facility or office	Name of health care professional that treated you

ALL OF THE QUESTIONS ON THIS PAGE REFER TO THE HEALTH CARE PROFESSIONAL ABOVE.

PHONE ( ) -	PATIENT ID# (if known)

MAILING ADDRESS

CITY	STATE/Province	ZIP/Postal Code	COUNTRY (if not USA)

Dates of Treatment (within the last 12 months)

1. Office, Clinic or Outpatient visits	2. Emergency Room Visits List the most recent date first	3. Overnight Hospitals Stays
First Visit _____ Last Visit _____ Next Scheduled Appointment (if any) _____	A _____ B _____ C _____	A. Date in _____ Date out _____ B. Date in _____ Date out _____ C. Date in _____ Date out _____

What medical conditions were treated or evaluated?

What treatment did you receive for the above conditions? (Do not describe medicines or tests in the box.)

Check the boxes below for any tests this provider performed or sent you to **within the last 12 months,** or has scheduled you to take. Please give the dates for past and future tests. If you need to list more tests, use **Section 11 - Remarks** on the last page.

☐ Check this box if no tests by this provider or at this facility.

KIND OF TEST	DATES OF TESTs	KIND OF TEST	DATES OF TESTs
☐ EKG (heart test)		☐ EEG (brain wave test)	
☐ Treadmill (exercise test)		☐ HIV Test	
☐ Cardiac Catheterization		☐ Blood Test (not HIV)	
☐ Biopsy (list body part)		☐ X-Ray (list body part)	
☐ Hearing Test		☐ MRI/CT Scan (list body part)	
☐ Speech/Language Test			
☐ Vision Test		☐ Other (please describe)	
☐ Breathing Test			

If you do not have any more doctors or hospitals to describe, go to Section 6 on page 8.

SECTION 5 - MEDICAL TREATMENT (continued)

5.G. Tell us who may have medical records covering the **last 12 months** about any of your physical or mental conditions(s) **(including emotional or learning problems)**. This includes doctors offices, hospitals (including emergency room visits), clinics, and other health care facilities. Tell us about your next appointment if you have one scheduled.

Name of facility or office	Name of health care professional that treated you

ALL OF THE QUESTIONS ON THIS PAGE REFER TO THE HEALTH CARE PROFESSIONAL ABOVE.

PHONE ( ) -	PATIENT ID# (if known)

MAILING ADDRESS

CITY	STATE/Province	ZIP/Postal Code	COUNTRY (if not USA)

Dates of Treatment (within the last 12 months)

1. Office, Clinic or Outpatient visits	2. Emergency Room Visits	3. Overnight Hospitals Stays
First Visit _____	List the most recent date first. A. _____	A. Date in _____ Date out _____
Last Visit _____	B. _____	B. Date in _____ Date out _____
Next Scheduled Appointment (if any) _____	C. _____	C. Date in _____ Date out _____

What medical conditions were treated or evaluated?

What treatment did you receive for the above conditions? (Do not describe medicines or tests in the box.)

Check the boxes below for any tests this provider performed or sent you to **within the last 12 months**, or has scheduled you to take. Please give the dates for past and future tests. If you need to list more tests, use **Section 11 - Remarks** on the last page.

☐ Check this box if no tests by this provider or at this facility.

KIND OF TEST	DATES OF TESTs	KIND OF TEST	DATES OF TESTs
☐ EKG (heart test)		☐ EEG (brain wave test)	
☐ Treadmill (exercise test)		☐ HIV Test	
☐ Cardiac Catheterization		☐ Blood Test (not HIV)	
☐ Biopsy (list body part)		☐ X Ray (list body part)	
☐ Hearing Test		☐ MRI/CT Scan (list body part)	
☐ Speech/Language Test			
☐ Vision Test		☐ Other (please describe)	
☐ Breathing Test			

If you do not have any more doctors or hospitals to describe, go to Section 6 on page 8.

~ 53 ~

If you are under age 18, Skip to Section 11 - Remarks on the last page.

SECTION 6 - OTHER MEDICAL INFORMATION
Complete only if you are age 18 years old or older

6. Does anyone else have medical information about your physical or mental condition(s) (including emotional and learning problems) **covering the last 12 months,** or are you scheduled to see anyone else? (This may include places such as workers' compensation, vocational rehabilitation, insurance companies who have paid you disability benefits, prisons, attorneys, social service agencies and welfare.)

☐ YES (Complete the following information.)   ☐ NO (Go to SECTION 7.)

NAME OF ORGANIZATION	PHONE NUMBER ( ) -

MAILING ADDRESS			
CITY	STATE/Province	ZIP/Postal Code	COUNTRY (if not USA)

NAME OF CONTACT PERSON	CLAIM NUMBER (if any)

Date First Contact (in last 12 months)	Date Last Contact (in last 12 months)	Date Next Contact (if any)

Reasons for Contacts

If you need to list other people or organizations use Section 11 - Remarks on the last page and give the same detailed information as above for each one you list.

SECTION 7 - MEDICINES

7. Are you now taking, or have you taken **in the last 12 months**, any prescription or non-prescription medicines?

☐ YES (Complete the following information. Look at your medicine containers.) if

☐ NO (Go to SECTION 8.)

NAME OF MEDICINE	IF PRESCRIBED, GIVE NAME OF DOCTOR	REASON FOR MEDICINE

If you need to list other medicines use Section 11 - Remarks on the last page

~ 54 ~

SECTION 8 - EDUCATION AND TRAINING
Complete only if you are age 18 years old or older

8.A. Have you received any education since your last disability decision? (See date at top of Page 1.)

☐ YES (Complete the information below.)   ☐ NO go to question **8.B** below

If Yes, what year did you last attend any school?

Please describe the education you received:

8.B. Have you received any type of specialized job, trade, or vocational training since your last disability decision? (See date at top of Page 1.)

☐ YES (Complete the information below.)   ☐ NO

NAME OF TRAINING FACILITY		PHONE ( ) -	
MAILING ADDRESS			
CITY	STATE/Province	ZIP/Postal Code	COUNTRY (if not USA)
TYPE OF PROGRAM		Date Completed (or scheduled to be completed)	

If you need to list other education information or training facilities use Section 11 - Remarks on the last page and give the same detailed information as above

SECTION 9 - VOCATIONAL REHABILITATION, EMPLOYMENT, OR OTHER SUPPORT SERVICES
Complete only if you are age 18 years old or older

9.A. Since the date of your last medical disability decision (see date on top of Page 1) have you participated, or are you participating, in:

- an individualized work plan with an employment network under the Ticket to Work Program
- an individualized plan for employment with a vocational rehabilitation agency or any other organization
- a Plan to Achieve Self-Support (PASS)
- an Individualized Education Program (IEP) through a school (if a student age 18-21); or
- any program providing vocational rehabilitation, employment services, or other support services to help you go to work?

☐ YES (Complete the information below.)   ☐ NO (Go to Section 10)

NAME OF ORGANIZATION OR SCHOOL			
NAME OF COUNSELOR, INSTRUCTOR, OR JOB COACH		PHONE NUMBER ( ) -	
MAILING ADDRESS			
CITY	STATE/Province	ZIP/Postal Code	COUNTRY (if not USA)

9.B. When did you start participating in the plan or program?

~ 55 ~

SECTION 9 - VOCATIONAL REHABILITATION, EMPLOYMENT, or OTHER SUPPORT SERVICES (continued)
Complete if you are age 18 years old or older

9.C. Are you still participating in the plan or program?

☐ YES. I am scheduled to complete the plan or program on

☐ NO. I completed the plan on _____ (date to be completed)
(date completed)

☐ NO. I stopped participating in the plan before completing it because

9.D. What types of services, tests, or evaluations were provided (for example, intelligence or psychological testing, vision or hearing test, physical exam, work evaluations, or classes?)

If you need to list another plan or program use Section 11 - Remarks on the last page and give the same detailed information as above

---

SECTION 10 - DAILY ACTIVITIES
Complete only if you are age 18 years old or older

10.A. Describe what you do in a typical day (for example, I get up around 7 A.M., take a shower, eat breakfast, etc.)

If you need more space, go to Section 11 - Remarks on the last page

10.B. Do you use an assistive device (for example, eye glasses, hearing aids, braces, canes, crutch(es), walker, wheelchair, service animal)?

☐ Always   ☐ Sometimes   ☐ Never

If ALWAYS OR SOMETIMES, please describe what kind, when, and how you use it.

If you need more space, use SECTION 11 - Remarks on the last page

10.C. Do you have hobbies or interests?

☐ YES   ☐ NO

If YES, please describe what they are and how much time you spend doing them.

If you need more space, use Section 11 - Remarks on the last page

~ 56 ~

SECTION 10 - DAILY ACTIVITIES (continued)
Complete only if you are age 18 years old or older

10.D. Do you ever have difficulty doing any of the following? (Please explain any "Yes" answers.)

Dressing	☐ Yes	☐ No
Bathing	☐ Yes	☐ No
Caring for hair	☐ Yes	☐ No
Taking medicines	☐ Yes	☐ No
Preparing meals	☐ Yes	☐ No
Feeding self	☐ Yes	☐ No
Doing chores (inside/outside house)	☐ Yes	☐ No
Driving or using public transportation	☐ Yes	☐ No
Shopping	☐ Yes	☐ No
Managing money	☐ Yes	☐ No
Walking	☐ Yes	☐ No
Standing	☐ Yes	☐ No
Lifting objects	☐ Yes	☐ No
Using arms	☐ Yes	☐ No
Using hands or fingers	☐ Yes	☐ No
Sitting	☐ Yes	☐ No
Seeing, hearing, or speaking	☐ Yes	☐ No
Concentrating	☐ Yes	☐ No
Remembering	☐ Yes	☐ No
Understanding or following directions	☐ Yes	☐ No
Completing tasks	☐ Yes	☐ No
Getting along with people	☐ Yes	☐ No

~ 57 ~

SECTION 11 - REMARKS

Please write any additional information you did not give in earlier parts of this report. If you did not have enough space in the sections of this report to write the requested information, please use this space to tell us the additional information requested in those sections. Be sure to show the section to which you are referring.

_____
_____
_____
_____
_____
_____
_____
_____
_____
_____
_____
_____
_____
_____
_____
_____
_____
_____
_____
_____
_____
_____
_____
_____
_____
_____

Date Report Completed (month, day, year)

~ 58 ~

This form will resemble the initial disability application. The form features some of the following questions:

Section 1

This section is basic information about who you are, your address, telephone number, etc. (With regards to the telephone number you supply, we strongly urge you to use one phone and that is a phone that only you will answer. It is best not to rely on anybody for messages or take the chance of possible misstatements by anyone else who answers your phone.)

Section 2

This is the Contact Section asking for a friend or relative who can speak about your condition. When supplying the name of someone, you have to make sure that this person is careful with their language. They could say something that could damage your case without even thinking that they have. An example is that your friend might want to make you look like a religious person and say you go to church, when in fact you go once in a while and don't stay for very long because it's hard in your condition to do so. They say you can take care of yourself very well and live very well when in fact you live in a small space and microwave all of your food. (One possible way around this issue would be to insert you don't want to bother your friends, and that you are a private person who doesn't share these matters with other people.)

If you are not the person completing the form, it asks for the contact information for that person.

Section 3

Now it's onto information regarding your medical conditions. Make sure you provide the complete list of diagnoses your medical providers have given you. List each and every problem you have that prevents you from doing any kind of work. You can add more conditions on the last page of the form in (Section 11) or write on the last line in this section "see attached" and add at the end of the form a piece of paper marked "section 11" and complete the list of your problems. Remember to include all of your physical, cognitive, and emotional issues, no matter how small, even if you don't think they're important. Social Security may deem them important.

Section 4

This Section refers to work. If you have been working a full-time job and haven't notified Social Security or you're on a trial work period, you will have problems. Often, Claimants get employment from relatives in what is known as a "sympathetic employment situation." Basically, nobody else will hire you but a friend or relative, and they've made what would be considered more than a reasonable accommodation to help you work.

Social Security is not asking what you actually do on the job. Many times, however, beneficiaries like to explain their job. Do not overstate what you actually do on the job. People tend to over-inflate their job responsibilities. If you must explain, don't be the Claimant who says they're responsible for everything at a trade show, when in fact, you were just standing at or sitting in a booth. Don't say you were in charge of marketing when the marketing consisted of simply posting on a social media platform. The more you say you are capable of doing, the more you will prevent yourself from keeping your benefits. You need to be honest in your assessment of your job duties, but this is not the time for your ego to lead the way.

We strongly recommend you attach a statement from your employer stating how he/she has made accommodations for you in order to help you out.

Keep Your Benefit Tip:

Do not rely upon Social Security to contact anyone. Help them do their job, by giving them the evidence that they need to make a favorable decision for you.

The Agency needs to see that you are not able to work in a competitive environment.

Section 5

The agency now devotes over six pages to learn what type of medical treatment you have had since you became disabled. And it's crucial to keeping your benefits. Remember when we suggested that you get a spiral notebook and keep track of your medical treatment and that you get copies of your records and get physical capacity forms completed on a regular basis? This is the day all of your record-keeping pays a huge dividend!

Now is the time you can help both Social Security and yourself. We believe you should simply write in Section 5 "see attached," start a separate piece of paper for each medical provider you have seen and attach all of the medical records you have from that medical provider.

You want it to be easy for Social Security to review all of your medical treatment and then come to only one conclusion – that you are disabled. By providing all of your medical records, you will save a lot of time in the process. Social Security will not have to contact your medical providers and wait for them to hopefully respond.

Social Security does not have the resources to continually contact medical providers, and they have no way of knowing if all of your records have been provided. Only you know that. Remember to separate each different medical provider so The Agency can easily see all of them.

If you are ambitious, you might want to put tabs for each appointment you had with each provider. If you have seen a lot of doctors, this makes a great visual for the amount of medical care you have been receiving. And, if you haven't been to a doctor much, it will still make it easier for Social Security to go through your records.

If you have had your medical providers complete the different forms we have made available for you in the back of this book, (or the detailed forms provided in Volume 3), attach them to the medical records. Place the completed form as the first page(s) in the group of records for each provider. The SSA will be able to then see the doctors' opinions and look at the medical records which support their conclusions.

Keep Your Benefit Tip:

Help Social Security help you. Make your claim one that is easy for them to decide and one for them to want to work up because it's organized and it can then be moved off of their desk.

Remember to also include a printout of all of the medications you have taken since you became disabled, a record of any support groups you have been part of and a list of any dietary supplements you are using to help your problems.

Keep Your Benefit Tip:

Complete the form thoroughly. It might be a good idea to have a close family member or friend review the form before you submit to SSA.

Keep Your Benefit Tip:

It is very helpful if you can attach your medical records to the forms being submitted to Social Security. You want to make it as easy as possible for Social Security to review and award your claim with continued benefits.

You are entitled to submit any updated medical evidence directly to the SSA. Just bear in mind that the SSA may also obtain your records by writing to your treatment physicians and/or facilities. This is a similar process to your original case. Usually, the SSA only reviews your activities and records for the 12 months immediately preceding the notice.

Did You Know That?

The agency can investigate and examine the evidence anytime after you are initially approved for benefits.

Under the new rules for submitting evidence in a disability case, you are required to submit all relevant evidence. This means that you must submit evidence even if it is not favorable to you.

If you are aware of unfavorable evidence against you, attack the issue head on. Medical providers sometimes are not clear in their record keeping. If your medical provider has noted your condition has improved, ask that provider to explain in your record if it has improved enough for you to work. Ask the medical provider if they can point to test results or examinations that support their conclusion why you can or cannot work.

Many times, the SSA focuses in on the words where the medical provider has said your condition has improved, so be ready to demonstrate that it is great that you are better, but it's not enough to do any kind of work.

There are limits to language, so you want to make any medical provider statement as clear as possible, and you should always have in the records language that can explain any improvement.

Keep Your Benefit Tip:

We recommend that every time you go to a medical provider you ask for a copy of your record. It could save you $$.

You should also obtain the records at the time they're noted at each medical provider appointment. This helps cut down the costs of getting a copy later. Also, a lot of times, for a number of reasons, when you seek your records later, the records you receive are not complete. When you ask for your records at the end of your appointment, you might receive resistance from the care provider, but it's not hard to make a photocopy of a few pages at the time you are in the office.

From a business standpoint, make the case that it is more cost effective for the provider to simply print what they have put into the electronic record during your examination, instead of having to process a medical release, find the records and do the accounting involved in paying for records. It's really just an easy click or two on a computer when you are leaving the facility. So, insist they do it for you.

Also, as we've suggested many times, we recommend you get a printout of your medications from your pharmacy once per year. This, too, should be submitted to the SSA.

You should also attach a printout of the possible side effects of your medications. Normally, there is a list of the side effects with the paperwork you get when you receive your medication, include these side effects with the records you submit.

Make sure the medical provider writes down all of your symptoms. It is very hard to remember visits years after they have taken place or try to look through receipts for visits. This is why you need your spiral notebook.

The Facts:

Treating Medical Sources used to be given the greatest weight as evidence...but not anymore...

CONSULTATIVE EXAMINATION

The SSA may send you out for a Consultative Examination from an independent physician selected by The Agency. If you can get your treating doctor to provide the information the SSA is seeking, you may be able to avoid this examination. You should make every effort to get your doctor to provide the information. Nobody knows you better, and it will be the most complete examination.

The Facts:

Having your treating doctor provide all requested information from SSA may mean you can avoid a request for a Consultative Examination.

If you receive a notice from Social Security to attend a Consultative Examination, immediately see if you can get one of your treating providers to supply the information the SSA feels it's lacking. Contact the person at the SSA who is handling your case and offer to provide the information. If you get resistance, remind the person you are talking with that you are saving the SSA money by not having to pay for a Consultative Examination. If you still have a problem, request to speak to a supervisor.

If you do go to a Consultative Examination, go with a prepared list of the medical problems you have and make sure you tell the consultative examiner about all of them. Also, specifically request that the doctor who is examining you, note your problems and ask that he/she address each and every one you have told them about. It is a stressful situation, and you may forget to mention one of your problems. Also, talk about the side effects of any medications you have and if they are affecting you. We recommend you bring a print out of all of the medications you have been taking for the last twelve months.

We have found that many times the Consultative Examinations are hurried. We recommend that you check the type of doctor who performs the examinations to make sure that their area of expertise coincides with what they have been hired to examine you for. Also, make notes as to the amount of time the doctor spends with you and what actual tests he/she performs.

If you have problems communicating with the doctor, due to language or other difficulties, note this. If you believe that the Consultative Examiner did not do a complete exam, forward to Social Security a written letter detailing the problems you encountered during the examination.

Some might say it's better to wait until the report comes in and is not favorable to point out the problems you had during the exam. We believe that if there's a problem, you should be upfront when it occurs. That way, it doesn't look like sour grapes after you've received a bad report.

The Facts:

With new rules relating to Consultative Examinations, they have greater weight as evidence than they used to. Before, you could rely on your treating doctor to have a greater weight of evidence than a Consultative Exmination. This may no longer be the case.

If you have been good about getting your records from your treating medical providers, we recommend you bring a copy to the Consultative Exam and ask the examiner to review those records. If he/she disagrees with the conclusions of your treating doctor, ask them to explain why in a short exam period he/she knows better than the doctor who has been taking care of you for years. Ask the Consultative Examiner to explain in his/her report why they disagree with test results.

If the doctor does not review your records or does this in a few seconds, this is something that you should write to the SSA about. There is no question that your treating medical provider is the best source to accurately determine your medical condition. But with the new rules, you need to demonstrate that the Consultative Examination is not as complete as your treating physician.

CHAPTER 5

HOW SOCIAL SECURITY DECIDES WHETHER OR NOT YOU ARE STILL DISABLED

At this point, it's time to explain how Social Security makes its decision as to whether or not you are still disabled. We can't even begin to count the number of times that somebody has told us they can't do the work they **_used_** to do. Keep in mind though that the bottom line is **_proving you are not able to do any type of work._** It makes no difference whether or not anyone will hire you. It only matters whether or not you are capable of working.

The Medical Improvement Standard

The SSA cannot terminate disability benefits unless it first finds substantial evidence of improvement in the individual's impairment(s) enabling him/her to engage in employment. Congress enacted MIRS in response to dissatisfaction with the Administration's use of CDRs to terminate large numbers of beneficiaries in the early 1980s.

The objective of a CDR is to determine whether the current beneficiary has experienced any recovery to lessen the medical severity of the disabling impairments. Also, it aims to uncover whether or not any medical improvement permits a beneficiary to perform substantial gainful activity/employment.

To make this assessment, the SSA utilizes a "comparison point date." In most cases, the comparison point date will probably be the date you were awarded disability or when your last CDR was performed.

The Social Security Advisory Board appointed an independent panel to review the CDR process, including the medical improvement standard. In a report released in December 2014, this panel recommended that the SSA retain the use of the standard. An interesting point that the panel discovered, however, was that disability examiners reported insufficient training in this area and that coding errors made it difficult to understand the CDR adjudicators' use of different exceptions.

If there is no evidence of medical improvement, there will be no cessation of benefits. There are, however, a few instances in which benefits can terminate even when there is no evidence of medical improvement:

 Advances in medical technology that enables you to engage in substantial gainful activity (SGA).

 New or improved diagnostic techniques/assessments that demonstrate the impairment was not as severe as it was when the initial determination was made.

 Significant evidence that shows the previous approval of benefits was made in error.

What Medical Improvement Will Generate a Termination of Benefits?

For the SSA to determine that an adult is no longer disabled, according to the medical improvement standard, the answer must be "yes" to the following three questions:

1. Has there been medical improvement since the most recent comparison point date?
2. Is the medical improvement related to the ability to work?
3. Due to the medical improvement, can the individual perform SGA?

The claim examiner must determine if the medical improvement is related to your ability to work. What does this mean? Essentially, it asks whether your residual functional capacity (RFC) has increased.

Residual functional capacity is not the easiest of concepts to understand. A thumbnail definition is that when you take into account all of the symptom(s) your medical condition(s) creates, including pain, the side effects of any medications and both your physical and mental limitations, how do these conditions impact what you can do in a work setting?

In other words, it's your functional capacity to do basic work activities. Under the law, disability is defined, in part, as the inability to do any substantial gainful activity by reason of any medical determinable physical or mental impairment(s). In determining whether you are disabled under the law, the SSA must measure, therefore, how and to what extent your impairment(s) has affected your ability to do work. They do this by looking at how your functional capacity for doing basic work activities has been affected.

Basic work activities are the abilities and aptitudes necessary to do most jobs. Included are exertional abilities such as walking, standing, pushing, pulling, reaching and carrying, and nonexertional abilities and aptitudes such as seeing, hearing, speaking, remembering, using judgment, dealing with changes and dealing with both supervisors and fellow workers.

A person who has no impairment(s) would be able to do all basic work activities at normal levels; he or she would have unlimited functional capacity to do basic work activities.

Depending on its nature and severity, an impairment will result in some limitation to the functional capacity to do one or more of these basic work activities. Diabetes, for example, can result in circulatory problems which could limit the length of time a person could stand or walk and damage to his or her eyes as well, so that the person also has limited vision.

What a person can still do despite an impairment is called his or her residual functional capacity. How the residual functional capacity is assessed is discussed in more detail in § 404.1545. Unless an impairment is so severe that it is deemed to prevent you from doing substantial gainful activity (see §§ 404.1525 and 404.1526), it is this residual functional capacity that is used to determine whether you can still do your past work or, in conjunction with your age, education and work experience, any other work.

Keep in mind that the following factors will work against you: the more skills you have, the better education you have, the younger you are and the more you are physically able to do.

We encourage you to remember that you are trying to prove you are not able to do any type of work.

As an illustration, let's say you have a cardiovascular disability that limits you to sedentary work. After a groundbreaking heart operation, however, your condition vastly improved and your RFC is raised to "capable of performing light work." (Part of the disability statute has appendixes that refer to different types of work, some of which are "sedentary," "light," etc.) Since your RFC increased from sedentary to light work, the SSA would consider this medical improvement "related to your ability to work."

There are other times in which your disability can medically improve but it does not change your RFC. In these cases, your benefits continue without interruption because you have the same exertional and employment limitations.

Social Security takes many factors into account when determining if you can work, such as whether or not you meet a medical listing and whether your combination of problems equals a medical listing. (Medical listings are listings of impairments that describe each major body system, impairments severe enough to prevent an individual from doing any gainful activity. Part A of the Listing of Impairments contains medical criteria that apply to the evaluation of impairments.) Your age, education and work background also come into play.

We have included at the end of this book two general residual functional capacity forms. One form is for physical problems. The other is for mental problems. These are the general forms that will be helpful. (In one of the companion volumes that goes along with this book, you will find a more complete list of forms for your medical provider to complete that is disease-specific and tied in more closely to the exact language Social Security is looking for to detail the exact medical criteria you must meet to be qualified under their listing of impairments.)

Exceptions to the Medical Improvement Standard (Group I exceptions):

The SSA does not need to show that your impairment has medically improved if:

- You are working over the substantial gainful activity (SGA) level
- You are participating in a vocational training program that makes it possible for you to return to work
- A new method for evaluating your condition shows you are not disabled
- There was an error in the initial determination and you should not have been found disabled

Two examples of this concept are:

Example 1:

You were found to be disabled because the limitations imposed on you by your impairment allowed you to only do work that was at a sedentary level of exertion. Your prior work experience was work that required a medium level of exertion. Your age and education at the time would not have qualified you for work that was below this medium level of exertion. In the period since you were awarded benefits, you enrolled in and completed a specialized training course which qualifies you for a job in data processing as a computer programmer. On review of your claim, current evidence shows that there is no medical improvement and that you can still do only sedentary work. As the work of a computer programmer is sedentary in nature, however, you are now able to engage in substantial gainful activity.

Example 2:

You were previously entitled to benefits because the medical evidence and assessment of your residual functional capacity showed you could only do light work. Your prior work was considered to be heavy in nature and your age, education and the nature of your prior work qualified you for work which was no less than medium in exertion. The current evidence and residual functional capacity show there has been no medical improvement and that you can still do only light work. Since you were originally entitled to benefits, your vocational rehabilitation agency enrolled you in and you successfully completed a trade school course so that you are now qualified to do small appliance repair. This work is light in nature, so when your new skills are considered, you are now able to engage in substantial gainful activity even though there has been no change in your residual functional capacity.

Exceptions to Being Capable of Performing SGA (Group II exception)

The SSA can cease benefits following a CDR even without having to show that you can engage in SGA. These are some examples of instances that are referred to as Group II Exceptions:

- ☐ Committed fraud
- ☐ Failed to cooperate with the disability review
- ☐ Cannot be located
- ☐ Did not follow treatment or failed to follow the doctor's prescribed treatment

CHAPTER 6

WHAT IF YOUR BENEFITS ARE TERMINATED?

As noted, a CDR can result in the cessation of benefits. If your benefits are terminated based on medical improvement, you will continue receiving benefits for just two months following the termination date. If you fail to cooperate or respond to notices, however, the result will be the immediate cessation of benefits (without a two-month grace period).

Social Security does not care that you were away visiting family, attending a funeral, helping a sick person or even if you were in the hospital. Have a backup person to collect your mail on a regular basis. If you become sick or are not at the address where you receive your mail, ignoring your mail is no longer an option for you.

Note: Again, as a reminder, the SSA will not contact you by email. Do not let yourself fall into one of the many email scams out there.

On a rare occasion, the SSA will call you, but never to let you know your benefits are being terminated. Always be cautious if you receive a call from the SSA. It's a good idea to always contact your local Social Security office, or call Social Security's toll-free Customer Service number at 1-800-772-1213, 7 a.m. to 7 p.m., Monday through Friday, to verify a call's legitimacy. (Those who are deaf or hard-of-hearing can call Social Security's TTY number at 1-800-325-0778.)

What to do if your benefits are terminated...

First, you will receive a letter from the SSA. The letter will contain a notice informing you that your benefits have been terminated. The notice has the following essential information:

1. Reasoning for the termination
2. Right to appeal information (You have 60 days from the receipt of notice to submit a Request for Reconsideration)
3. Information on how to maintain benefits during the appeals process (Request for continuing benefits must be completed and sent back to SSA within 10 days from the date of receipt of the notice SSA Form 795)

If you disagree with the determination and cessation of benefits, you must first submit a Request for Reconsideration Form (SSA-789-U4). This document is straightforward and requires you to fill out basic biographical information. The Request for Reconsideration Form also provides you a brief opportunity to assert why you disagree with the CDR decision.

We recommend you outline for the SSA all of the medical evidence you have submitted that supports a finding that you are disabled. It might seem like you are doing the same thing over and over again, but you always want to be making the point that you are not able to work and why.

It is imperative that this form be filed **within 60 days** from the date you receive your notice. The sooner you do this, the better. There are and have historically been large backlogs of cases at Social Security, so you want to move forward as quickly as you can.

Keep Your Benefit Tip:

There is no reason to delay your appeal. We recommend that you gather all of the evidence you have been collecting since the date of your decision and make a copy of that evidence and submit it with your request for reconsideration. The use of the forms attached to this book, for the different impairments you may have will prove very useful.

We cannot stress enough that, if you elect to continue benefits during the reconsideration period, you must file within 10 days from the receipt of notice. Along with your Request for Reconsideration, you must include a written and signed statement to the SSA requesting the maintenance of benefits. The form to file to request continuing benefits is the Benefit Continuation Election Statement SSA Form 795 (https://ssa-795-fillable-form.pdffiller.com).

The SSA sometimes misplaces forms you send them, so your appeal should be sent in with a way to prove that they have received it. You can use the USPS Certified Mail Return Receipt option, UPS or Fed Ex, or you can go to the district office yourself and get them to stamp a copy for you that the document has been filed. Don't be surprised if a clerk at the district office doesn't want to sign that your request was hand-delivered. Just ask for a supervisor.

You never know when it will be critical for you to prove that you made a timely filing of any appeal. Keep a copy of everything you send to the SSA! Always prepare to prove you filed your papers with the SSA.

Keep Your Benefit Tip:

With any correspondence sent to SSA get delivery confirmation. Also keep a copy of everything you have sent in.

Word of caution

If you choose to continue benefits in the interim, you will most likely have to repay the value of the benefits if you lose your appeal. The SSA is currently engaged in practices of recovery for overpayment of benefits that reach out past your death and impact living relatives. So just know there is a possibility the money you get will have to be repaid at some point if you lose, and it can not only impact you but your heirs as well.

Also, there have been instances when the SSA has gone after your relatives to collect past money due through IRS refunds. The Agency, at one point, did suspend the collection of past due benefits from tax refunds, but it appears that this will be a yearly decision and you never know what The Agency's position will be.

In addition to the Request for Reconsideration, you will be required to fill out an SSA-3441-BK, Disability Report—Appeal. Here is a link to that form, https://www.ssa.gov/forms/ssa-3441.pdf (There is a copy of this form in this book). The purpose of this form is to supply and update medical contact information for the SSA. This form is similar to your initial disability report filed way back when you first applied for disability. Therefore, even if you have previously submitted this form, you will need to complete it again.

Go back and look at the advice we provided about completing SSA- 454 -BK (Continuing Disability Review Report). Especially the advice we have provided about the following sections: work (Section 4) and medical treatment (Section 5). Report any changes since you filed your last report. Use the same format to submit medical records that you used in Section 5 of the Continuing Disability Review Report. Also, put on a separate piece of paper an outline of the exhibits/information/records you have filed with your Continuing Disability Review Report.

If your case ever gets to the Federal District Court, you want to have what is known as a complete record. This is where that spiral notebook you bought to track your medical appointments becomes very valuable. If for some reason you did not do a complete job with your Continuing Disability Review Report, don't be lazy now. Put together all of your medical evidence. Your claim depends on it.

Don't forget to include any changes in medications and new test results. Include any and all medical information that you feel is pertinent to your condition and which supports your inability to work. Point out to Social Security that this is either a new medical provider or additional evidence since you last submitted information to The Agency. Also, double check your medical providers' contact information. Sometimes, facilities or doctors relocate. If the physician has relocated, you need to find out if your medical records went with the doctor or stayed at his/her previous facility.

Keep Your Benefit Tip:

We recommend that you take advantage of this opportunity to advocate for yourself. (You should take every bite out of the appeal apple that you can). When you go, you should bring a copy of every document you have submitted and make sure that whoever you talk to has those exact same records in front of him/her. If not, hand them a copy. Also, you should dress appropriately for this meeting. Wear business casual and refrain from wearing jewelry or loud prints.

While your request is pending, you are permitted to schedule a face-to-face interview with Disability Determination Services (DDS). A disability determiner will review your file, and a reversal of the termination of benefits is possible. If the determination is upheld and there is no reinstatement of benefits, your file will be sent to a Disability Hearing Officer (DHO) for a hearing.

We believe in taking every possible bite out of the appeal apple so schedule this face-to-face. Come prepared with a complete copy of your file for the Officer you are meeting. Hopefully, he/she will have your file, but if not, how nice for you to be able to hand over whatever the Officer will need.

When you go to the hearing, dress for success. Even though today's world is very casual, dress up. If you are a guy, dockers/khakis or dress pants are fine. No jeans for either a man or a woman. Wear colors that are well-received such as white, pale colors of yellow or light blue. Try to stay away from black as it has a lot of negative connotations. For a woman, our preference is to wear a dress. But if not, a blouse and pants are fine. We do not recommend wearing any jewelry. If you normally wear makeup, we also suggest not wearing any. Just look like yourself. You do not want to cover up the flaws that make you look sick. You want to dress as middle of the road as possible – not your best clothes, but not your worst either. The old expression 'a picture is worth a thousand words' is something to keep in mind. You want to present yourself as a likable person who really needs the Social Security Disability Benefit.

Who Analyzes your CDR?

Disability Hearing Officers (DHOs) are officials trained in how to analyze and review the medical and legal issues most relevant to CDR cases. The SSA's objective in requiring that CDR appeals be heard first by DHOs instead of an Administrative Law Judge (ALJ) is an attempt to decrease the caseload on ALJs' dockets.

DHO Hearing

You will be sent a letter informing you of the time and location of your DHO hearing. The letter also inquires if you will have any witnesses testify on your behalf as well as whether or not you will have an attorney present.

Keep Your Benefit Tip:

It is a good idea to give yourself plenty of extra time to get to the hearing office promptly. Plan on arriving at least 45 minutes before the hearing is scheduled to start. It will inevitably be one of those mornings when you are already running late and you hit that big traffic jam on the highway! It is not a bad idea to make a dry run to the office the day before to know exactly where the office is located and on what floor in the building.

When you arrive at the office, check in with the administrative assistant and wait for your name to be called. Try not to be nervous. Your hearing with the DHO will be casual and almost feel like a conversation. The hearing is not conducted in a courtroom. They're typically held in a private conference room.

At the start of the hearing, the DHO will describe how the hearing will work. He/she will likely give you the opportunity to explain why your medical condition has not improved and why your benefits should continue.

Keep Your Benefit Tip:

Come with prepared notes to outline your position. When speaking, look directly at the DHO, make eye contact and be succinct.

Come prepared to the hearing. **Nothing succeeds like preparation**. Practice what you want to say in front of friends. Make your points in a succinct way. Make it easy for the DHO to understand why you are still disabled.

Remember that the hearing officer is not your friend. If anything, in today's climate, whether Social Security admits it or not, there is a bit of a bias for denying claims.

There was an expression in World War II "loose lips sink ships," and this certainly applies here. Be careful what you say and respond only to the question that is being asked. Do not offer more.

The DHO might ask you questions such as how do you spend your day (e.g. watching TV, going for a walk, social activities). This is what is known as Activities of Daily Living (ADL). Remember, too, it is not just what you can do once or twice in a day, it is what you would be able to do on a fairly-regular basis during an 8-hour work day. They are simply looking to see how your condition affects your life in a number of areas and how these limitations (if any) would hamper you from performing a job.

Did You Know That?

The more you say you are able to do the more you can hurt yourself. It is very important not to overstate your ability to do anything. There is a big difference between being able to lift 5 lbs. vs. 10 lbs. Being off by just that five-pound amount, increases your capacity to lift by 50%!

Ask yourself when was the last time you lifted a 5-lb sack of sugar or potatoes and was it difficult? Could you lift this amount of weight a couple of times every hour for an 8-hour work day? When was the last time you walked 4 blocks (1/2 mile)? If you have not done any of these physical activities, there is probably a reason you have not done so, and the most likely answer is, is that it is difficult for you to do.

Do not be coaxed into giving an answer that is a guess. If you don't know or don't remember, those are good answers. If the hearing officer suggests possible answers, just keep saying you don't remember (if you don't know or remember). Maybe you don't remember because you rarely do some of the activities of daily living that most people do, and the reason for that is you are not able to do such activities anymore.

The DHO will also most likely ask about your most recent medical treatments and your past work history. Have a copy of what you have already submitted to the SSA on the desk in front of you. Refer to those records for both your medical treatment and your work history. This is a document that you took time to create, so rely on it.

Explain to the DHO that you want to make sure you are accurate and not trust your memory because everybody's memory is far from perfect, especially if you are in a stressful situation like a hearing to keep your SS Benefits.

Keep Your Benefit Tip:

Do not overly embellish your job skills or what you actually did on the job. The more skills you have the more it works against you. We have in the past routinely seen clients that say they can do more than they can because they are embarrassed. Park your embarrassment and ego at the door and just be honest as to your limitations.

Issues to Raise with DHO

1. If new medical evidence is not in your file, it is important to bring this to the attention of the DHO. You want to make sure that the DHO is not using old or incomplete medical records to make a determination.

Keep Your Benefit Tip:

Prior to your hearing, it is a good idea to visit your local DDS field office to review your file. It will provide you the chance to check if all the medical records you want are in the file and if anything is missing.

---

2. Did a Disability Determination Doctor review your file? You have the right to request that a medical professional review your file along with the DHO. We suggest that you only do this if you do not have any evidence to support your case. If you have been keeping up with seeing a doctor, your medical records should be more than complete to support a finding of disability.

Keep Your Benefit Tip:

Make sure the credentials of the medical reviewer are attached. You can then check to see if it is the correct specialty and if the doctor is still licensed. How old the doctor is can impact his/her cognitive abilities.

---

3. Focus on what improvements the SSA believes you have experienced that now permit you to return to work. This allows you to raise medical evidence or doctors' opinions that specifically counter the SSA's claim that you are medically improved to the point where you can hold a job.

Keep Your Benefit Tip:

If you can, get your treating source doctor to state in writing that he/she disagrees with the consultative exam or conclusion of the SS doctor.

---

4. Are there any errors in the DDS documents?

You might be surprised to see another person's name appear as part of your file, or a report from a medical source might refer to a person of a different sex or not even address your medical problems but rather someone else's.

Keep Your Benefit Tip:

Make sure all of the documents in the file are for your claim and make sure the documents are dated and signed.

What if the decision doesn't go in your favor?

After the hearing concludes, it will take approximately 3-7 weeks to receive a written decision in the mail. The decision will inform you of whether or not your benefits have been reinstituted and, if not, why that decision was reached.

If the DHO upholds the termination, you can make a Request for a Hearing in front of an ALJ (Administrative Law Judge). There is a 60-day deadline to appeal your decision.

Remember to respond to all SSA correspondence quickly. As with the previous denial of benefits, you can keep your benefits coming as long as you ask in writing within 10 days.

Steps to Request a Hearing Before an ALJ

You are required to submit several forms (links to which are located in our Forms Library at the back of the book):

1. HA-501-U5- Request for Hearing by Administrative Law Judge (ALJ) Form 789-U4. You will provide, for what will seem like the thousandth time, basic biographical and personal data. Also, you can briefly write why you believe the DHO's determination was incorrect and include any new medical evidence that you may have obtained since the DHO hearing.

2. SA-3441-BK- Disability Report Appeal

This is similar to the disability report you have filled out before. You should include any new information not found in your old report. Once again, reference the advice we provided on completing the Continuing Disability Review Report. The same information and tips will apply here.

3. SSA-827- Authorization for Source to Release Information to the SSA.

This form is a medical release that permits the SSA to request medical records from your providers. Do not sign an authorization, however, that does not have a termination date. If the form does not have one, write underneath your signature that the release to provide medical information expires one year from the date you have signed the release. Never allow it to be valid for more than one year.

After you have submitted the forms, you will be placed in a waiting pool to schedule your hearing before an ALJ.

Note: Due to huge backlogs of cases, individual wait times vary, and occasionally, it can take one year or more for your court date. The delays at the hearing office level have been a problem for a long period of time. We do suggest every three to four months you contact the hearing office to make sure your claim has not been lost. Note the date you called and who you spoke with. If you have been to the doctor since the last time you called, go ahead and submit the new evidence to Social Security. There is no reason to wait. Try to get somebody at the hearing office to take a look at the new evidence and ask them to make a favorable ruling for you.

The hearing will be similar to your first hearing when you were initially awarded benefits (if you had to go to a hearing). If you did not have go to a hearing to be awarded benefits, the format will be similar to the hearing you had with the DHO, only this time with an Administrative Law Judge.

Do not be in awe of the Judge. He/she puts on their clothes the same way you do. Also, you are a taxpayer, so these people work for you. There should be mutual respect between both you and the Judge. If for some reason you feel you are not receiving the respect you deserve, speak up. The case is being recorded, so you would want to make a record of poor treatment by the Judge.

If you do say something, treat the Judge in the same way you would want to be treated, with courtesy, but speak your mind! This can be a reason that a bad decision can be overturned.

Don't walk out of the hearing feeling you should have said something. This is your opportunity to tell your story.

The ALJ will likely ask questions to determine your medical treatments and how your symptoms affect your ability to work. The questions will be very similar to those that were asked at the DHO.

We urge you to come prepared with an opening statement in which you've written down the reasons why you feel you cannot do any type of work. Reference the medical records that support you not being able to do any kind of work. Try to be as specific as possible when noting these medical records, use the dates of the treatment. And it is really great if you can point out to the Judge what exhibit it is in your file.

This is your hearing, and you have the right to speak and for as long as you need to. Do not allow yourself to be rushed. You have waited a long time for this hearing. Take advantage of your opportunity to speak. At no future point in this process will you ever be allowed to testify again.

If you are not sure of a question that is being asked of you, don't guess what it is, ask the Judge to repeat him/herself. It is the responsibility of the Judge to ask a question that you can understand. If you answer, it is assumed you understand the question. If you do not completely understand what is being asked of you and you go ahead and give an answer, you may be shooting yourself in the foot.

If an ALJ returns an unfavorable decision, there are still more appeal options at your disposal. You can appeal to the Appeals Council, and then if you are still denied at that level, you can take your claim to Federal District Court.

Review of Appeals Levels:

1. DDS Interview
2. DHO Hearing
3. Request for Hearing in front of an ALJ

4. Appeals Council
5. Federal Court

The Facts:

It is advisable to attempt to find an attorney for appeals levels 4-5, but be prepared to go it alone.

CHAPTER 7

IN CONCLUSION...

Throughout this book, we've given you a variety of tips, tools and strategies for success to help you keep your Social Security Disability Benefits.

We love connecting with our readers and continuing the journey with you. Please join us on Facebook at:

https://www.facebook.com/jerry.zivic.1 and
https://www.facebook.com/JerryZivicCommentator/

And, we look forward to sharing more with you in Volumes 2 and 3 which are coming soon!

Volume 2 will trace the history of CDR development, the reasons it came about and the legislative route that this program has taken, along with statistics tracking the growth of CDRs. You'll be able to draw your own conclusions as to what the Social Security Administration is trying to accomplish.

Volume 3 will provide disease specific medical forms for you to have your medical provider complete. These forms are easy for your medical provider to complete. Basically, all that is required is for your provider to write in a few words. No narrative is needed which makes it very user-friendly for your medical provider. These forms are Social Security Disability specific which will help Social Security come to the correct decision in your case.

Sincerely –

Jerry and Aaron

ACKNOWLEDGMENTS

We would like to thank the people who contributed to this work in many different ways…

Judy Zivic was a tireless supporter of the concept, offered never-ending support, provided her keen business acumen, language skills, brilliant mind and unmatched ability to get everything coordinated that needed to get done to get these volumes published. Without her support, these books would have never been written. A BIG THANK YOU!

Also, we would like to acknowledge and thank D. D. Scott for helping bring the book to life and pulling all of the different pieces together to get a book published.

Leann Spofford's assistance in raising awareness of this book was invaluable.

To Stu Auslander for his always wise counsel, Linda Rubin for her keen eye and Susan Nilon for her encouragement to complete this book, we also say thank you.

FORMS LIBRARY

Mental RFC

MENTAL RESIDUAL FUNCTIONAL CAPACITY EVALUATION

PATIENT:_____

SOCIAL SECURITY
#:_____
DATE OF
BIRTH:_____

Dear Doctor:

In addition to the information provided in your narrative report, please complete Items 1 through 12 by circling the appropriate word and items 13 through 17 by filling in the blank. It is essential that your answers be based on your estimate of claimant's current psychiatric impairment and not on non-medical factors, such as availability of job openings or hiring practices of employers. However, it is also essential that the assessment be of ability to perform these activities over a sustained period of time in a full or part time work setting.

Please indicate Degree of Limitation based on the following definitions:

NONE: No impairment in this area.

SLIGHT: Suspected impairment, which marginally affects ability to function.

MODERATE: Impairment which imposes more than marginal, but less than a serious effect on the ability to function.

MARKED: An impairment, which seriously affects ability to function.

EXTREME: Extreme impairment of ability to function over a sustained period of time.

UNKNOWN: Insufficient evidence.

The patient's sustained ability in an 8-hour workday, 5 days a week, to:

1. Understand, remember, and carry out an extensive variety of technical and/or complex job instructions:

NONE
SLIGHT
MODERATE
MARKED
EXTREME
UNKNOWN

2.Understand, remember, and carry out detailed but uncomplicated job instructions:

NONE
SLIGHT
MODERATE
MARKED

EXTREME
UNKNOWN

3.Understand, remember, and carry out simple one or two-step job instructions (assess all three cumulatively):

NONE
SLIGHT
MODERATE
MARKED
EXTREME
UNKNOWN

4.Interact appropriately with supervisors and supervisory demands in a competitive job setting:

NONE
SLIGHT
MODERATE
MARKED
EXTREME
UNKNOWN

5.Interact appropriately with co-workers in a competitive job setting:

NONE
SLIGHT
MODERATE
MARKED
EXTREME

UNKNOWN

6.Deal appropriately with the public:

NONE
SLIGHT
MODERATE
MARKED
EXTREME
UNKNOWN

7.Maintain sustained concentration and attention:

NONE
SLIGHT
MODERATE
MARKED
EXTREME
UNKNOWN

8.Respond appropriately to customary work pressures five days a week in a routine work setting:

NONE
SLIGHT
MODERATE
MARKED
EXTREME
UNKNOWN

9.Care appropriately for his/her own grooming and hygiene:

NONE
SLIGHT
MODERATE
MARKED
EXTREME
UNKNOWN

10.Perform adaptive activities such as cleaning and cooking:

NONE
SLIGHT
MODERATE
MARKED
EXTREME
UNKNOWN

11.Initiate and participate in activities required for daily living outside the home, (e.g. going shopping, using a post office, or taking public transportation):

NONE
SLIGHT
MODERATE
MARKED
EXTREME
UNKNOWN

12.Travel unaccompanied outside of one's immediate living:

NONE
SLIGHT
MODERATE
MARKED
EXTREME
UNKNOWN

13.Is the patient's mental status likely to result in decompensation under the stress of a competitive full-time job in a non-sheltered environment? Yes _____ No _____

If yes, please explain:

14.If the patient suffers from substance abuse or addiction (alcohol or drugs), will he/she be able to control or refrain from the use of the substance while working at a competitive non-sheltered job? Yes _____ No _____

If no, please explain:

15.In each question above marked "unknown", state what evidence or tests could provide this data:

16.Duration of impairment:
Will the limitation listed above last for 12 months or
longer? Yes _____ No _____

If the limitations already have lasted for over 13 months,
when did these limitations begin?

17.Has there been a diagnosis of the patient's impairment?
Yes _____ No _____
If yes, give the DSM-III classification:

Date Report Completed:
_____
Signature of Physician:
_____
Physician Name: _____
Address: _____
Telephone: _____
Specialty: _____

Physical RFC

PHYSICAL CAPACITIES EVALUATION

Patient Name:

_____

Social Security #:

_____

Date of Birth:

_____

Please complete the following evaluation of your patient's ability to perform work activities. Indicate the level of work your patient can perform despite his or her limitations. This assessment must be based on objective clinical observations and/or laboratory findings. The levels of work activity at any levels of work activity used on this form are defined on page three.

To be able to perform the work activity at any level you patient must be able to perform substantially all of the requirements for work at that level for a sustained 8-hour day, five days a week. For example, to perform sedentary work, an individual must be able to sit 6 to 8 hours without constant breaks to stand and stretch.

Please describe the patient's abilities with respect to the following:

A.

If lifting/carrying affected by impairment? Yes_____ No_____

If yes, how many pounds can the individual lift and/or carry? _____

Maximum occasionally (from very little up to 1/3 of an 8-hour day? _____

Maximum frequently (from 1/3 to 2/3 of an 8-hour day)? _____

What are the medical findings that support this assessment?

_____

_____

B.

Are standing/walking affected by impairment? Yes_____ No_____

If yes, how many hours in an 8-hour workday cam the individual stand and/or walk: total? _____ without interruption? _____

What are the medical findings that support this assessment?

_____

_____

C.

Is sitting affected by impairment? Yes_____ No_____

If yes, how many hours in an 8-hour workday cam the individual sit: total? _____ without interruption? _____

What are the medical findings that support this assessment?

_____

_____

D.

How often can the individual perform the following postural activities?

Frequently Occasionally Never

(Frequently=1/3 to 2/3 of an 8-hour workday; Occasionally= very little to 1/3 of an 8-hour workday)

Climb _____ _____ _____
Balance _____ _____ _____
Stoop _____ _____ _____
Crouch _____ _____ _____
Kneel _____ _____ _____
Crawl _____ _____ _____
Operate foot controls _____ _____ _____
Reach above right shoulder level _____ _____
_____
Reach above left shoulder level _____ _____
_____
Gross manipulations (Simple Grasping) _____
_____ _____
Fine manipulations (wire, small tools) _____ _____
_____
What are the medical findings that support this assessment?
_____
_____
E.
Are the following physical functions affected by the
impairment?
Yes No
Reaching _____ _____
Handling _____ _____
Feeling _____ _____
Pushing/Pulling _____ _____
Seeing _____ _____
Hearing _____ _____
Speaking _____ _____
What are the medical findings that support this assessment?
_____
_____
F.

Are there environmental restrictions caused by the impairment?

Yes No

Heights _____ _____
Moving machinery _____ _____
Temperature extremes _____ _____
Chemicals _____ _____
Dust _____ _____
Noise _____ _____
Fumes _____ _____
Humidity _____ _____
Vibrations _____ _____
Other _____ _____

How do the checked restrictions affect the individual's activities?

_____
_____

What are the medical findings that support this assessment?

_____
_____

G.

State any other work-related activities which are affected by the impairment, and indicate how the activities are affected. What are the medical findings that support this assessment?

_____
_____

_____
_____

Date Report Completed:

_____

Signature of Physician:
_____
Physician Name: _____
Address: _____
Telephone: _____
Specialty: _____

SEDENTARY WORK:
Sedentary work entails lifting 10 pounds maximum and occasionally lifting or carrying such articles as dockets (e.g. files), ledgers and small tools. Although a sedentary job is defined as one which involves sitting, a certain amount of walking and standing is often necessary in carrying out job duties. Jobs are sedentary if walking and standing are required and other sedentary criteria are met. An individual cannot perform sedentary work if (s)he is unable to sit hours without standing.

LIGHT WORK:
Light work entails lifting 20 pounds maximum with frequent lifting or carrying of objects weighing up to 10 pounds. Even though the weight lifted may be only a negligible amount, a job is in this category when it requires walking or standing to a significant degree, or when it involves sitting most of the time with a degree of pushing and pulling of arm or leg controls. To be considered capable of performing a full or wide range of substantially all of the forgoing activities. The functional capacity to perform light work includes the functional capacity to perform sedentary work.

MEDIUM WORK:
Medium work entails lifting 50 pounds maximum with frequent lifting or carrying of objects weighing up to 50 pounds. The functional capacity to perform medium work includes the capacity to perform work at all of the lesser functional levels.

HEAVY WORK:
Heavy work entails lifting 100 pounds maximum with frequent lifting or carrying of objects weighing up to 50 pounds. The functional capacity to perform heavy work includes the capacity to perform work at all of the lesser functional levels.

VERY HEAVY WORK:
Very heavy work entails lifting objects in excess of 100 pounds with frequent lifting or carrying of objects weighing up to 50 pounds or more. The functional capacity to perform very heavy work includes the capacity to perform work at all of the lesser functional levels.

SSA FORMS

Short Form
Form (SSA-455)

Social Security Administration
Disability Update Report
Information and Completion Instructions

Why We Are Writing To You Now	The Social Security Administration must regularly review the cases of people getting disability benefits to make sure they are still disabled under our rules. It is time for us to review this case. Enclosed is a **Disability Update Report** for you to answer to update us about you for the person for whom you are the representative payee) your health and medical conditions, any recent work activity, or any recent training.
What To Do First	**Please read** the following information, **and** the instructions for completing the report form, **before** you answer the questions.
When to Respond	Please complete the report, **sign it** and send it to us in the enclosed envelope within **30 days**. If there is no return envelope with the report please send the signed report to us at:
	Social Security Administration
	P.O. Box 4550
	Wilkes-Barre, PA 18767-4550
What We Do With Your Answers	We consider the information you give us together with the information in your claim record to decide if we need to do a full medical review. After we receive the completed report, we will notify you whether or not we need to do a full medical review.
If You Need Help To Answer The Report	It is important that information you give us is accurate. We have tried to make report questions easy to understand and answer. But, if you find that you do not understand a question or questions, please contact us, your authorized representative, a social service agency, your doctor or clinic, or some other person you trust.
If You Need To Contact Us	If you need to contact us, please call us toll-free at **1-800-772-1213** or TTY for the hearing impaired at **1-800-325-0778**. We can answer most questions over the telephone. If you prefer to visit or call one of our offices, please use the 800 number to get the local office address and telephone number. Please have the Disability Update Report with you if you call or visit an office. It will help us answer your questions. Also, if you plan to visit an office, you should call ahead to make an appointment. This will help us serve you.
We May Need To Contact You	Sometimes, we may need more information from you. If so, we will try to call you. If you do not have a telephone, please give us a number where we can leave a message for you. Please print the telephone number in the section provided on the back of the report form.
If We Don't Hear From You	If you do not complete and return the report promptly, or tell us why you cannot respond, we may stop sending payments to you. If it is necessary to stop your payments, we will send you another letter telling you what we plan to do.

If We Do A Full Medical Review	If we decide to do a full medical review of your case, you can give us any information which you believe shows that you are still disabled, such as medical reports and letters from your doctors about your health. Then, we look at all your information in your case, including the new information you give us, and decide whether you continue to be disabled under our rules.
Appeals And Continued Benefits	When we review your case, we may find that you are no longer disabled under our rules, and your payments may stop. If your payments stop, you can appeal our decision or you can ask us to continue to make payments while you appeal.
If You Want To Work	Do you want to work, but worry about losing your payments or Medicare before you can support yourself? We want to help you go to work when you are ready. But, work and earnings **may** affect your benefits. Your local Social Security office can tell you more about work incentives, and how work and earnings can affect your benefits.
The Privacy And Paperwork Reduction Acts	**Collection and Use of Personal Information** Sections 205(a) and 1631(a)(1) and 1b) of the Social Security Act, as amended, and Social Security regulations at 20 CFR 404.1589 and 416.989 authorize us to collect this information. We will use the information you provide to further document your claim and permit us to continue to make a continuing disability.

The information you furnish on this report is voluntary. However, failure to provide us with the requested information could prevent us from making an accurate and timely decision on your claim.

We rarely use this information you supply for any purpose other than for reviewing your claim for Social Security benefits. However, we may use it for the administration and integrity of Social Security programs. We may also disclose information to another person or to another agency in accordance with approved routine uses, which include but are not limited to the following:

    1. To enable a third party or an agency to assist Social Security in establishing rights to Social Security benefits and/or coverage;

    2. To comply with Federal laws requiring the release of information from Social Security records (e.g., to the Government Accountability Office and Department of Veterans Affairs);

    3. To make determinations for eligibility in similar health and income maintenance programs at the Federal, State, and local level; and

    4. To facilitate statistical research, audit, or investigative activities necessary to assure the integrity and improvement of Social Security programs.

We may also use the information you provide in computer matching programs. Matching programs compare our records with records kept by other Federal, State, or local government agencies. Information from these matching programs can be used to establish or verify a person's eligibility for Federally-funded or administered benefit programs and for the repayment of payments or delinquent debts under these programs.

A complete list of routine uses for this information are available in our Systems of Records Notices entitled, Claims Folders Systems and 60-0089 and the Master Beneficiary Record 60-0090. These notices, additional information regarding this form, and information about our programs and systems are available on-line at www.socialsecurity.gov or at your local Social Security office.

Paperwork Reduction Act Statement - This information collection meets the requirements of 44 U.S.C. § 3507, as amended by section 2 of the Paperwork Reduction Act of 1995. You do not need to answer these questions unless we display a valid Office of Management and Budget (OMB) control number. The OMB control number for this collection is 0960-0511. We estimate that it will take 10 minutes to read the instructions, gather the facts, and answer the questions. **Send only comments relating to our time estimate above to: SSA, 6401 Security Blvd, Baltimore, MD 21235-6401.**

GENERAL INSTRUCTIONS - HOW TO COMPLETE "SCANNABLE" FORMS	The Disability Update Report is a scannable form which can be "read" electronically. To help us process your report, **please follow these instructions when you answer the questions on the report form:**

1. USE BLACK INK OR A #2 PENCIL.
2. KEEP YOUR NUMBERS, LETTERS, AND "X'S" INSIDE THE BOXES.
3. NUMBERS: Try to make your numbers look like these:

$$0\ 1\ 2\ 3\ 4\ 5\ 6\ 7\ 8\ 9$$

4. LETTERS: Print in CAPITALS. Try to make your letters look like these:

$$A\ B\ C\ D\ E\ F\ G\ H\ I\ J\ K\ L\ M$$
$$N\ O\ P\ Q\ R\ S\ T\ U\ V\ W\ X\ Y\ Z$$

5. MONEY AMOUNTS: Show dollars only. Do not use dollar signs ($), and do not show cents. For example, show $1,540.30 like this:

Dollars Only, No Cents

$$0\ 1\ ,\ 5\ 4\ 0$$

6. DATES: Put a number in each box. For example, show September 9, 2003, like this:

Month   Year

$$0\ 9\quad 0\ 3$$

7. THE REPORT PERIOD: The report period is the period of time for which we need information. It is described at the top of the report form to the right of your name, and again in questions 1 through 6. Usually, the report period is the last 24 months, but it may be less. **It is important that you keep the report period in mind when answering the questions.**

HOW TO FILL OUT THE REPORT FORM

QUESTION 1.a. - Have You Worked?	If you have not worked during the report period, place an "X" in the box below "NO", and go on to question 2. If you have worked, mark the box below "YES", and answer question 1.b.
QUESTION 1.b. - When You Worked And Your Monthly Earnings	**Describe your most recent work activity first.** Print the months and years you began and ended working in the boxes under "Work Began" and "Work Ended. **If you are working now**, print the current month and year in the first set of boxes under "Work Ended. Print your gross monthly earnings for the periods you worked in the boxes.
QUESTION 2 - School Or Work Training	Place an "X" in the box below "YES" if you have attended school and/or a training program during the report period; otherwise, mark the box below "NO". This could include high school equivalency programs, college courses, vocational evaluation or retraining programs, but generally would not include group therapy or hobbies.

QUESTION 3 - Can You Work?	Tell us if you have discussed with your doctor whether you can return to any kind of work, and if so, whether the doctor told you that you can return to work, even if the work permitted is less physically demanding and/or less stressful than your usual work. **Place an "X" in only 1 box.**
QUESTION 4 - How Is Your Health?	We want to know how your overall health now compares to what it was at the beginning of the report period. You may feel that your health has gotten worse, has improved, or you may feel that your health is about the same and has not gotten better or worse. **Place an "X" in only 1 box.**
QUESTION 5 - Treatment By A Doctor Or Clinic	A "doctor or clinic" can include treatment such as evaluations, checkups, counseling, providing prescriptions or medicine by a doctor, visiting nurse, family health center, psychologist, licensed counseling service, physical therapist, a chiropractor or other licensed health provider. Treatment may be provided in person or by telephone or other contact.
How To Answer Question 5.a.	If you have not been treated by a doctor or clinic during the report period, place an "X" in the box below "NO", and go on to question 6. If you have gone to a doctor or clinic during the report period, mark the box below "YES", and answer question 5.b.
Question 5.b. - Reason For The Visit	**Please start with the most recent visit and then work backwards in time.** Print as much information as will fit, but keep a space between each word. Try to use the most important or key word(s), such as **ARTHRITIS** or **BAD BACK**, or **HYPERTENSION** or **HIGH BLOOD**. Your medical bills or doctor can provide a short, accurate description.
Date of Visit	Print the month and year you were treated. Complete all 4 boxes. For example, print September 10, 2003, as **09 03**.
	NOTE: If needed, use the "REMARKS" section on side 2 of the form.
QUESTION 6.a - Have You Been Hospitalized Or Had Surgery?	Place an "X" in the box below "NO" if you have not been hospitalized or not had surgery during the report period. If you have been hospitalized or had surgery during the report period, then place an "X" in the box below "YES" and answer question 6.b.
Question 6.b. - Reason For Treatment	**Please report your most recent treatment first and then work backwards in time.** Try to provide the most important information. Keep a space between each word. Your medical bills or doctor can provide short, accurate words.
Date of Treatment	Print the month and year you were hospitalized or had surgery. Be sure to use all four spaces. **If you were hospitalized more than one month**, print last month you were hospitalized.
	NOTE: If needed, use the "REMARKS" section on side 2 of the form.
Remarks Section	If you need more room to answer questions 1.b., 5.b. and/or 6.b., or there are any other facts or statements you want us to consider, place an "X" in the box and write in this section. If necessary, use an extra piece of paper.
Signature, Date and Telephone Sections	Please sign the report form as you usually sign your name. Please provide a telephone number where you can be reached during the day.

Disability Update Report

DATE

Social Security Administration P.O. Box, Wilkes-Barre, PA 18767.

FORM APPROVED
OMB No. 0960-0511

PAYEE'S NAME AND ADDRESS	REPORT PERIOD	
	From	To The Present
	BENEFICIARY	
Pay	TELEPHONE NUMBER	CLAIM NUMBER

Please be sure to **use black ink or a #2 pencil to print your answers.** Also, read the enclosed instructions before completing the form. Finally, remember that when answering the questions, the **"REPORT PERIOD" for which we need information about you is from** _____ **to the present.** If you have any questions, call 1-800-772-1213 or TTY for the hearing impaired at 1-800-325-0778.

---

1. a. Since _____ have you worked for someone or been self-employed? ⟶   YES ☐   NO ☐

b. If you answered "YES" to 1.a., please complete the information below.

	WORK BEGAN		WORK ENDED		MONTHLY EARNINGS
	Month	Year	Month	Year	Before Only Deduction
Most Recent Work 1.	☐	☐	☐	☐	$ ☐ ☐
2.	☐	☐	☐	☐	$ ☐ ☐
3.	☐	☐	☐	☐	$ ☐ ☐

---

2. Have you attended any school or work training program(s) since _____ ?   YES ☐   NO ☐

---

3. Since _____ to the present. *(Please place an 'X' in one box only):*

☐ my doctor and I have not discussed whether I can work

☐ my doctor told me I could not work

☐ my doctor told me I could work

---

4. Place an 'X' in only one box which best describes your health now as compared to _____

☐ BETTER   ☐ SAME   ☐ WORSE

5. a. Have you gone to a doctor or clinic for treatment
(including evaluations, checkups, counseling,
prescriptions, or medicine) since _____ ?

    YES ☐   No ☐

  b. If you answered "YES" to 5.a., please list:

	Reason For Visit	Month	Year
Most Recent Visit 1.			
2.			
3.			

6. a. Have you been hospitalized or had surgery
since _____ ?

    YES ☐   No ☐

  b. If you answered "YES" to 6.a., please list:

	Reason For Hospitalization or Surgery	Month	Year
Most Recent 1.			
2.			
3.			

REMARKS: If you use this space to further answer questions 1. through 6.,
place an "X" in the box to the right and print on the lines below. ☐

_____
_____
_____
_____

I declare under penalty of perjury that I have examined all the information on this form,
and on any accompanying statements or forms, and it is true and correct to the best of
my knowledge. I understand that anyone who knowingly gives a false or misleading
statement about a material fact in this information, or causes someone else to do so,
commits a crime and may be sent to prison, or may face other penalties, or both.

| SIGN HERE ➤ | TODAY'S DATE |
| | TELEPHONE NUMBER (include Area Code) |

Form SSA-1556 ("E-SM (10-2015)

Long Form
Form (SSA-454)

CONTINUING DISABILITY REVIEW REPORT
SSA-454-BK

PLEASE READ THIS INFORMATION BEFORE COMPLETING THIS REPORT

The office that reviews your medical condition will use the information in this report. The information will help that office decide whether you are still disabled. Please complete as much of the report as you can.

IF YOU NEED HELP

You can get help from other people, such as a friend or family member. Please **do not** ask your health care provider to complete this report. If you cannot complete the report, a Social Security Representative will assist you. If you have an appointment, please have the completed report ready when we contact you.

Note: If you are assisting someone else with this report, please answer the questions as if that person were completing the report.

HOW TO COMPLETE THIS REPORT

- Print or write clearly.
- Include a ZIP or postal code with each address.
- Provide complete phone numbers, including area code. If a phone number is outside the United States, provide International Direct Dialing (IDD) code and country code.
- If you cannot remember the names and addresses of your health care providers, you may be able to get that information from the telephone book, Internet, medical bills, prescriptions, or prescription medicine containers.
- **ANSWER EVERY QUESTION**, unless the report indicates otherwise. If you do not know an answer, or the answer is "none" or "does not apply," please write "don't know," or "none," or "does not apply."
- Be sure to explain an answer if the question asks for an explanation or if you want to give additional information.
- If you need more space to answer any question, please use **Section 11 - Remarks**, on the last page to finish your answer. Write the number of the question you are answering.

YOUR MEDICAL RECORDS

If you have any of your medical records covering the last 12 months, send or bring them to our office with this completed report. Please tell us if you want to keep your records so we can return them to you. If you have a scheduled appointment for an interview, bring your medical records, your prescription medicine containers (if available), and the completed report with you.

YOU DO NOT NEED TO ASK DOCTORS OR HOSPITALS FOR ANY MEDICAL RECORDS THAT YOU DO NOT ALREADY HAVE. With your permission, we will request your records. The information that you give us on this report tells us where to request your medical and other records.

Form **SSA-454-BK** (07-2016) ef (07-2016) Destroy prior editions

The Privacy Act

Sections 205(a), 223(d), and 1631(e) (1) of the Social Security Act, as amended, authorize us to collect this information. The information you provide will be used to make a decision on the named claimant's claim. While giving us the information on this report is voluntary, failure to provide all or part of the requested information could prevent an accurate or timely decision on the named claimant's claim. We generally use the information you supply for the purpose of making decisions regarding claims. However, we may use it for the administration and integrity of Social Security programs. We may also disclose information to another person or to another agency in accordance with approved routine uses, which include but are not limited to the following: (1) to enable a third party or agency to assist Social Security in establishing rights to Social Security benefits and/or coverage, (2) to comply with Federal Laws requiring the release of information about Social Security records (e.g., to the Government Accountability Office and the Department of Veterans Affairs); (3) to make determinations for eligibility in similar health and income maintenance programs at the Federal, State, and local level; and, (4) to facilitate statistical research, audit, or investigative activities necessary to assure the integrity of Social Security programs.

We may also use the information you provide in computer matching programs. Matching programs compare our records with records kept by other Federal, State, or local government agencies. Information from these matching programs can be used to establish or verify a person's eligibility for Federally-funded or administered benefit programs and for repayment of payments or delinquent debts under these programs.

Additional information regarding this form, routine uses of information, and our programs and systems, is available on-line at www.socialsecurity.gov or at any local Social Security office.

The Paperwork Reduction Act

This information collection meets the requirements of 44 U.S.C. § 3507, as amended by section 2 of the Paperwork Reduction Act of 1995. You do not need to answer these questions unless we display a valid Office of Management and Budget control number. We estimate that it will take about 60 minutes to read the instructions, gather the facts, and answer the questions. You may send comments on our time estimate above to: SSA, 6401 Security Boulevard, Baltimore, MD 21235-6401. **Send only comments relating to our time estimate to this address, not the completed report.**

SEND OR BRING THE COMPLETED REPORT TO YOUR LOCAL SOCIAL SECURITY OFFICE, THE NEAREST U.S EMBASSY OR CONSULATE OFFICE. Office addresses are listed under U.S. Government agencies in your telephone directory or you may call 1-800-772-1213 (TTY 1-800-325-0778) for the address.

AFTER COMPLETING THIS FORM, REMOVE THIS SHEET AND KEEP IT FOR YOUR RECORDS.

Form **SSA-454-BK** (07-2010) ef (07-2010)

Form Approved
OMB No. 0960-0072

CONTINUING DISABILITY REVIEW REPORT

For SSA Use Only - Do not write in this box	Date of your last medical disability decision:

Claim Number _____   Number Holder _____

Type(s) of Case(s) (Check all that apply)	TITLE II	☐ DIB	☐ DWB	☐ CDB	☐ FZ	☐ ESRD	☐ HB
	TITLE XVI	☐ DI	☐ DS	☐ CC	☐ BI	☐ BS	☐ BC

If you are filling out this report for the disabled person, please provide information about him or her. When a question refers to "you", "your", or the "disabled person", it refers to the person receiving disability benefits.

SECTION 1- INFORMATION ABOUT THE DISABLED PERSON

1.A. NAME (first, middle initial, last)   **1.B.** SOCIAL SECURITY NUMBER

1.C. MAILING ADDRESS (Street or PO Box) Include apartment number if applicable

CITY	STATE/Province	ZIP/Postal Code	COUNTRY (if not USA)

1.D. DAYTIME PHONE NUMBER including area code, and the IDD and country codes if you live outside the USA or Canada

Phone number _____

☐ Check this box if you have a phone or a number where we can leave a message

1.E. Alternate Phone Number, including area code where we may reach you, if any

Alternate phone number _____

1.F. Can you speak and understand English?   ☐ YES ☐ NO

If no, what language do you prefer?
If you cannot speak and understand English, we will provide an interpreter, free of charge.

1.G. Have you used any other names on your medical or educational records in the last 12 months?
Examples are maiden name, other married names, or nickname.   ☐ YES ☐ NO

If yes, please list them here _____

SECTION 2 - CONTACTS

Give the name of a friend or relative (other than your doctors) we can contact who knows about your medical conditions, and can help you with your case.

2.A. NAME (first, middle initial, last)	**2.B.** Relationship to Disabled Person

2.C. MAILING ADDRESS (Street or PO Box) Include apartment number if applicable

CITY	STATE/Province	ZIP/Postal Code	COUNTRY (if not USA)

2.D. DAYTIME PHONE NUMBER (as described in 1.D. above)

_____

2.E. Can this person speak and understand English?   ☐ YES ☐ NO
If no, what language is preferred? _____

~ 119 ~

SECTION 2 - CONTACTS (continued)

2.F. Who is completing this report?

☐ The disabled person listed in 1.A. (Go to **Section 3 - Medical Conditions**)

☐ The person listed in 2.A. (Go to **Section 3 - Medical Conditions**)

☐ Someone else (Complete the rest of Section 2 below)

2.G. NAME (first, middle initial, last)	**2.H.** Relationship to Disabled Person

2.I. DAYTIME PHONE NUMBER (as described in 1.D. above)

2.J. MAILING ADDRESS (Street or PO Box) Include apartment number if applicable

CITY	STATE/Province	ZIP/Postal Code	COUNTRY (if not USA)

SECTION 3 - MEDICAL CONDITION(S)

3.A. If you are an adult (age 18 or older) list the physical and/or mental condition(s) (including emotional or learning problems) that limit your ability to work. **If you are completing this report for a child (under age 18)**, list the physical and/or mental condition(s) (including emotional and learning problems) that limit the child's ability to do the same things as other children the same age. **List each physical and/or mental condition separately.**

1

2

3

4

If you need more space go to Section 11 - Remarks on last page

3.B. What is your height without shoes? ____ feet ____ inches OR ____ centimeters (if outside USA)

3.C. What is your weight without shoes? ____ pounds OR ____ kilograms (if outside USA)

SECTION 4 - WORK
Complete only if you are age 14 years old or older

4. Since the date of your last medical disability decision have you worked? (see date at top of Page 1)

☐ YES (if yes, we may contact you for additional information) ☐ NO

SECTION 5 - MEDICAL TREATMENT

Within the last 12 months, have you seen a doctor or other health care professional or received treatment at a hospital or clinic, or **do you have a future appointment scheduled:**

5.A. For any **physical** conditions?

☐ YES ☐ NO

5.B. For any **mental** condition(s) **(including emotional or learning problems)**

☐ YES ☐ NO

If you answered "No" to both 5.A. and 5.B., go to Section 6 - Other Medical Information on page 8

~ 120 ~

SECTION 5 - MEDICAL TREATMENT (continued)

5.C. Tell us who may have medical records covering **the last 12 months** about any of your physical or mental condition(s) **(including emotional or learning problems)**. This includes doctors' offices, hospitals (including emergency room visits), clinics, and other health care facilities. Tell us about your next appointment, if you have one scheduled.

Name of facility or office	Name of health care professional that treated you

ALL OF THE QUESTIONS ON THIS PAGE REFER TO THE HEALTH CARE PROFESSIONAL ABOVE.

PHONE ( ) -	PATIENT ID# (if known)

MAILING ADDRESS

CITY	STATE/Province	ZIP/Postal Code	COUNTRY (if not USA)

Dates of Treatment (within the last 12 months)

1. Office, Clinic or Outpatient visits	2. Emergency Room Visits (List the most recent date first)	3. Overnight Hospitals Stays
First Visit _____	A _____	A. Date in _____ Date out _____
Last Visit _____	B _____	B. Date in _____ Date out _____
Next Scheduled Appointment (if any) _____	C _____	C. Date in _____ Date out _____

What medical conditions were treated or evaluated?

What treatment did you receive for the above conditions? (Do not describe medicines or tests in the box.)

Check the boxes below for any tests this provider performed or sent you to **within the last 12 months**, or has scheduled you to take. Please give the dates for past and future tests. If you need to list more tests, use **Section 11 - Remarks** on the last page.

☐ Check this box if no tests by this provider or at this facility.

KIND OF TEST	DATES OF TESTS	KIND OF TEST	DATES OF TESTS
☐ EKG (heart test)		☐ EEG (brain wave test)	
☐ Treadmill (exercise test)		☐ HIV Test	
☐ Cardiac Catheterization		☐ Blood Test (not HIV)	
☐ Biopsy (list body part)		☐ X-Ray (list body part)	
☐ Hearing Test		☐ MRI/CT Scan (list body part)	
☐ Speech/Language Test			
☐ Vision Test		☐ Other (please describe)	
☐ Breathing Test			

If you do not have any more doctors or hospitals to describe, go to Section 6 on page 8.

~ 121 ~

SECTION 5 - MEDICAL TREATMENT (continued)

5.D. Tell us who may have medical records covering **the last 12 months** about any of your physical or mental condition(s) **(including emotional or learning problems)** This includes doctors' offices, hospitals (including emergency room visits), clinics, and other health care facilities. Tell us about your next appointment, if you have one scheduled.

Name of facility or office	Name of health care professional that treated you

ALL OF THE QUESTIONS ON THIS PAGE REFER TO THE HEALTH CARE PROFESSIONAL ABOVE.

PHONE ( ) -	PATIENT ID# (if known)
MAILING ADDRESS	

CITY	STATE/Province	ZIP/Postal Code	COUNTRY (if not USA)

Dates of Treatment (within the last 12 months)

1. Office, Clinic or Outpatient visits	2. Emergency Room Visits List the most recent date first	3. Overnight Hospitals Stays
First Visit _____ Last Visit _____ Next Scheduled Appointment (if any) _____	A _____ B _____ C _____	A. Date in _____ Date out _____ B. Date in _____ Date out _____ C. Date in _____ Date out _____

What medical conditions were treated or evaluated?

What treatment did you receive for the above conditions? (Do not describe medicines or tests in the box.)

Check the boxes below for any tests this provider performed or sent you to **within the last 12 months**, or has scheduled you to take. Please give the dates for past and future tests. If you need to list more tests, use **Section 11 - Remarks** on the last page.

☐ Check this box if no tests by this provider or at this facility.

KIND OF TEST	DATES OF TESTs	KIND OF TEST	DATES OF TESTs
☐ EKG (heart test)		☐ EEG (brain wave test)	
☐ Treadmill (exercise test)		☐ HIV Test	
☐ Cardiac Catheterization		☐ Blood Test (not HIV)	
☐ Biopsy (list body part)		☐ X-Ray (list body part)	
☐ Hearing Test		☐ MRI/CT Scan (list body part)	
☐ Speech/Language Test			
☐ Vision Test		☐ Other (please describe)	
☐ Breathing Test			

If you do not have any more doctors or hospitals to describe, go to Section 6 on page 8.

~ 122 ~

SECTION 5 - MEDICAL TREATMENT (continued)

5.E. Tell us who may have medical records covering **the last 12 months** about any of your physical or mental condition(s) **(including emotional or learning problems)** This includes doctors' offices, hospitals (including emergency room visits), clinics, and other health care facilities. Tell us about your next appointment, if you have one scheduled.

Name of facility or office	Name of health care professional that treated you

ALL OF THE QUESTIONS ON THIS PAGE REFER TO THE HEALTH CARE PROFESSIONAL ABOVE.

PHONE ( ) -	PATIENT ID# (if known)

MAILING ADDRESS

CITY	STATE/Province	ZIP/Postal Code	COUNTRY (if not USA)

Dates of Treatment (within the last 12 months)

1. Office, Clinic or Outpatient visits	2. Emergency Room Visits List the most recent date first	3. Overnight Hospitals Stays
First Visit		
	A	A. Date in _____ Date out _____
Last Visit		
	B	B. Date in _____ Date out _____
Next Scheduled Appointment (if any)		
	C	C. Date in _____ Date out _____

What medical conditions were treated or evaluated?

What treatment did you receive for the above conditions? (Do not describe medicines or tests in the box.)

Check the boxes below for any tests this provider performed or sent you to take **within the last 12 months**, or has scheduled you to take. Please give the dates for past and future tests. If you need to list more tests, use **Section 11 - Remarks** on the last page.

☐ Check this box if no tests by this provider or at this facility.

KIND OF TEST	DATES OF TESTs	KIND OF TEST	DATES OF TESTs
☐ EKG (heart test)		☐ EEG (brain wave test)	
☐ Treadmill (exercise test)		☐ HIV Test	
☐ Cardiac Catheterization		☐ Blood Test (not HIV)	
☐ Biopsy (list body part)		☐ X-Ray (list body part)	
☐ Hearing Test		☐ MRI/CT Scan (list body part)	
☐ Speech/Language Test			
☐ Vision Test		☐ Other (please describe)	
☐ Breathing Test			

If you do not have any more doctors or hospitals to describe, go to Section 6 on page 8.

~ 123 ~

SECTION 5 - MEDICAL TREATMENT (continued)

5.F. Tell us who may have medical records covering **the last 12 months** about any of your physical or mental condition(s) **(including emotional or learning problems)**. This includes doctors' offices, hospitals (including emergency room visits), clinics, and other health care facilities. Tell us about your next appointment, if you have one scheduled.

Name of facility or office	Name of health care professional that treated you

ALL OF THE QUESTIONS ON THIS PAGE REFER TO THE HEALTH CARE PROFESSIONAL ABOVE.

PHONE ( ) -	PATIENT ID# (if known)

MAILING ADDRESS

CITY	STATE/Province	ZIP/Postal Code	COUNTRY (if not USA)

Dates of Treatment (within the last 12 months)

1. Office, Clinic or Outpatient visits	2. Emergency Room Visits (List the most recent date first)	3. Overnight Hospitals Stays
First Visit _____	A _____	A. Date in ____ Date out ____
Last Visit _____	B _____	B. Date in ____ Date out ____
Next Scheduled Appointment (if any) _____	C _____	C. Date in ____ Date out ____

What medical conditions were treated or evaluated?

What treatment did you receive for the above conditions? (Do not describe medicines or tests in the box.)

Check the boxes below for any tests this provider performed or sent you to take **within the last 12 months**, or has scheduled you to take. Please give the dates for past and future tests. If you need to list more tests, use **Section 11 - Remarks** on the last page.

☐ Check this box if no tests by this provider or at this facility.

KIND OF TEST	DATES OF TESTs	KIND OF TEST	DATES OF TESTs
☐ EKG (heart test)		☐ EEG (brain wave test)	
☐ Treadmill (exercise test)		☐ HIV Test	
☐ Cardiac Catheterization		☐ Blood Test (not HIV)	
☐ Biopsy (list body part)		☐ X-Ray (list body part)	
☐ Hearing Test		☐ MRI/CT Scan (list body part)	
☐ Speech/Language Test			
☐ Vision Test		☐ Other (please describe)	
☐ Breathing Test			

If you do not have any more doctors or hospitals to describe, go to Section 6 on page 8.

Form **SSA-454-BK** (07-2010) ef (07-2010)

SECTION 5 - MEDICAL TREATMENT (continued)

5.G. Tell us who may have medical records covering **the last 12 months** about any of your physical or mental condition(s) **(including emotional or learning problems)** This includes doctors offices, hospitals (including emergency room visits), clinics, and other health care facilities. Tell us about your next appointment, if you have one scheduled.

Name of facility or office	Name of health care professional that treated you

ALL OF THE QUESTIONS ON THIS PAGE REFER TO THE HEALTH CARE PROFESSIONAL ABOVE.

PHONE ( ) -	PATIENT ID# (if known)

MAILING ADDRESS

CITY	STATE/Province	ZIP/Postal Code	COUNTRY (if not USA)

Dates of Treatment (within the last 12 months):

1. Office, Clinic or Outpatient visits	2. Emergency Room Visits List the most recent date first	3. Overnight Hospitals Stays
First Visit _____ Last Visit _____ Next Scheduled Appointment (if any) _____	A _____ B _____ C _____	A. Date in ____ Date out ____ B. Date in ____ Date out ____ C. Date in ____ Date out ____

What medical conditions were treated or evaluated?

What treatment did you receive for the above conditions? (Do not describe medicines or tests in the box.)

Check the boxes below for any tests this provider performed or sent you to **within the last 12 months**, or has scheduled you to take. Please give the dates for past and future tests. If you need to list more tests, use **Section 11 - Remarks** on the last page.

☐ Check this box if no tests by this provider or at this facility.

KIND OF TEST	DATES OF TESTs	KIND OF TEST	DATES OF TESTs
☐ EKG (heart test)		☐ EEG (brain wave test)	
☐ Treadmill (exercise test)		☐ HIV Test	
☐ Cardiac Catheterization		☐ Blood Test (not HIV)	
☐ Biopsy (list body part)		☐ X-Ray (list body part)	
☐ Hearing Test		☐ MRI/CT Scan (list body part)	
☐ Speech/Language Test			
☐ Vision Test		☐ Other (please describe)	
☐ Breathing Test			

If you do not have any more doctors or hospitals to describe, go to Section 6 on page 8.

Form **SSA-454-BK** (07-2010) ef (07-2012)

SECTION 6 - OTHER MEDICAL INFORMATION
Complete only if you are age 18 years old or older

6. Does anyone else have medical information about your physical or mental condition(s) (including emotional and learning problems) **covering the last 12 months,** or are you scheduled to see anyone else? (This may include places such as workers' compensation, vocational rehabilitation, insurance companies who have paid you disability benefits, prisons, attorneys, social service agencies and welfare.)

☐ YES (Complete the following information.) ☐ NO (Go to SECTION 7.)

NAME OF ORGANIZATION	PHONE NUMBER ( ) -

MAILING ADDRESS

CITY	STATE/Province	ZIP/Postal Code	COUNTRY (if not USA)

NAME OF CONTACT PERSON	CLAIM NUMBER (if any)

Date First Contact (in last 12 months)	Date Last Contact (in last 12 months)	Date Next Contact (if any)

Reasons for Contacts

If you need to list other people or organizations use Section 11 - Remarks on the last page and give the same detailed information as above for each one you list.

SECTION 7 - MEDICINES

7. Are you now taking, or have you taken **in the last 12 months** any prescription or non-prescription medicines?

☐ YES (Complete the following information. Look at your medicine containers.)

☐ NO (Go to SECTION 8.)

NAME OF MEDICINE	IF PRESCRIBED, GIVE NAME OF DOCTOR	REASON FOR MEDICINE

If you need to list other medicines use Section 11 - Remarks on the last page

~ 126 ~

SECTION 8 - EDUCATION AND TRAINING
Complete only if you are age 18 years old or older

8.A. Have you received any education since your last disability decision? (See date at top of Page 1.)

☐ YES (Complete the information below.)   ☐ NO go to question **8.B** below

If Yes, what year did you last attend any school?

Please describe the education you received:

8.B. Have you received any type of specialized job, trade, or vocational training since your last disability decision? (See date at top of Page 1.)

☐ YES (Complete the information below.)   ☐ NO

NAME OF TRAINING FACILITY		PHONE ( ) -	
MAILING ADDRESS			
CITY	STATE/Province	ZIP/Postal Code	COUNTRY (if not USA)
TYPE OF PROGRAM		Date Completed (or scheduled to be completed)	

If you need to list other education information or training facilities use Section 11 - Remarks on the last page and give the same detailed information as above

SECTION 9 - VOCATIONAL REHABILITATION, EMPLOYMENT, OR OTHER SUPPORT SERVICES
Complete only if you are age 18 years old or older

9.A. Since the date of your last medical disability decision (see date on top of Page 1), have you participated, or are you participating, in:
- an individualized work plan with an employment network under the Ticket to Work Program;
- an individualized plan for employment with a vocational rehabilitation agency or any other organization;
- a Plan to Achieve Self-Support (PASS);
- an Individualized Education Program (IEP) through a school (if a student age 18-21); or
- any program providing vocational rehabilitation, employment services, or other support services to help you go to work?

☐ YES (Complete the information below.)   ☐ NO (Go to Section 10)

NAME OF ORGANIZATION OR SCHOOL			
NAME OF COUNSELOR, INSTRUCTOR, OR JOB COACH		PHONE NUMBER ( ) -	
MAILING ADDRESS			
CITY	STATE/Province	ZIP/Postal Code	COUNTRY (if not USA)

9.B. When did you start participating in the plan or program?

~ 127 ~

SECTION 9 - VOCATIONAL REHABILITATION, EMPLOYMENT, or OTHER SUPPORT SERVICES (continued)
Complete if you are age 18 years old or older

9.C. Are you still participating in the plan or program?

☐ YES. I am scheduled to complete the plan or program on _____
_____ (date to be completed)

☐ NO. I completed the plan on _____
(date completed)

☐ NO. I stopped participating in the plan before completing it because

9.D. What types of services, tests, or evaluations were provided (for example: intelligence or psychological testing, vision or hearing test, physical exam, work evaluations, or classes?)

If you need to list another plan or program use Section 11 - Remarks on the last page and give the same detailed information as above

---

SECTION 10 - DAILY ACTIVITIES
Complete only if you are age 18 years old or older

10.A. Describe what you do in a typical day (for example: I get up around 7 A.M., take a shower, eat breakfast, etc.)

If you need more space, go to Section 11 - Remarks on the last page

10.B. Do you use an assistive device (for example: eye glasses, hearing aids, braces, canes, crutch(es), walker, wheelchair, service animal)?

☐ Always   ☐ Sometimes   ☐ Never

If ALWAYS OR SOMETIMES, please describe what kind, when, and how you use it

If you need more space, use SECTION 11 - Remarks on the last page

10.C. Do you have hobbies or interests?

☐ YES   ☐ NO

If YES, please describe what they are and how much time you spend doing them.

If you need more space, use Section 11 - Remarks on the last page

Form **SSA-454-BK** (07-2010) ef (07-2010)

~ 128 ~

SECTION 10 - DAILY ACTIVITIES (continued)
Complete only if you are age 18 years old or older

10.D. Do you ever have difficulty doing any of the following? (Please explain any "Yes" answers.)

Dressing	☐ Yes	☐ No
Bathing	☐ Yes	☐ No
Caring for hair	☐ Yes	☐ No
Taking medicines	☐ Yes	☐ No
Preparing meals	☐ Yes	☐ No
Feeding self	☐ Yes	☐ No
Doing chores (inside/outside house)	☐ Yes	☐ No
Driving or using public transportation	☐ Yes	☐ No
Shopping	☐ Yes	☐ No
Managing money	☐ Yes	☐ No
Walking	☐ Yes	☐ No
Standing	☐ Yes	☐ No
Lifting objects	☐ Yes	☐ No
Using arms	☐ Yes	☐ No
Using hands or fingers	☐ Yes	☐ No
Sitting	☐ Yes	☐ No
Seeing, hearing, or speaking	☐ Yes	☐ No
Concentrating	☐ Yes	☐ No
Remembering	☐ Yes	☐ No
Understanding or following directions	☐ Yes	☐ No
Completing tasks	☐ Yes	☐ No
Getting along with people	☐ Yes	☐ No

~ 129 ~

SECTION 11 - REMARKS

Please write any additional information you did not give in earlier parts of this report. If you did not have enough space in the sections of this report to write the requested information, please use this space to tell us the additional information requested in those sections. Be sure to show the section to which you are referring.

Date Report Completed (month, day, year)

~ 130 ~

Request for Reconsideration Form (SSA-789-U4)

https://www.ssa.gov/forms/ssa-789.pdf

Page 1 of 2

OMB No. 0960-0349

REQUEST FOR RECONSIDERATION - DISABILITY CESSATION RIGHT TO APPEAR (SEE REVERSE SIDE FOR PAPERWORK/PRIVACY ACT NOTICE)	FOR SOCIAL SECURITY OFFICE USE ONLY

NAME OF CLAIMANT — SOCIAL SECURITY NUMBER

(DO NOT WRITE IN THIS SPACE)

NAME OF WAGE EARNER OR SELF-EMPLOYED PERSON (If different from Claimant) — SOCIAL SECURITY NUMBER

☐ FO Code _____

☐ Benefit Continuation

SPOUSE'S NAME AND SOCIAL SECURITY NUMBER (COMPLETE ONLY IN SUPPLEMENTAL SECURITY INCOME CASE)

☐ Foreign Language Notice _____

TYPE OF BENEFIT	DISABILITY			SSI		
	☐ WORKER	☐ WIDOW	☐ CHILD	☐ DISABILITY	☐ BLIND	☐ CHILD

I DO NOT AGREE WITH THE DETERMINATION TO STOP DISABILITY BENEFITS AND I REQUEST RECONSIDERATION.

My reasons are (reasons should relate to the basis for stopping disability benefits and be as specific as possible)
NOTE If the notice of the determination on your claim is dated more than 65 days ago, include your reason for not making this request earlier. Include the date on which you received the notice.

I AM SUBMITTING THE FOLLOWING ADDITIONAL INFORMATION (If "NONE" write "NONE")
(Attach additional page if needed)

CHECK BLOCK 1 AND THE STATEMENTS THAT APPLY OR CHECK BLOCK 2.

☐ 1 **I (and/or my representative) wish to appear** at a face-to-face disability hearing. The disability hearing will be with a person called a disability hearing officer and it will let me explain why I do not agree with the decision to stop benefits

☐ I need an interpreter at the disability hearing - Language _____

OR (If you need an interpreter, SSA will provide one at no cost to you)

☐ 2 **I do not wish to appear nor do I wish a representative to appear for me** at the disability hearing. I have been advised of my right to have a disability hearing. I understand that a disability hearing will give me a chance to present witnesses. It will also let me explain to the disability hearing officer why my disability benefits should not end. I understand that this chance to be seen and heard could help the disability hearing officer learn about the facts in my case. The disability hearing officer would give me a chance to have people who know about my condition give information and explain how my condition keeps me from working and restricts my activities. I have been told about my right to representation at the disability hearing, including representation by an attorney or other person of my choice. Although the above has been explained to me, I do not want to appear at a disability hearing, or have someone represent me at a disability hearing. I prefer to have the disability hearing officer decide my case on the evidence in my file, plus any evidence that I submit or that may be obtained by the Social Security Administration. I have been advised that if I change my mind, I can request a disability hearing prior to the writing of a decision in my case. In this case, I can make the request with any Social Security office.

I declare under penalty of perjury that I have examined all the information on this form, and on any accompanying statements or forms, and it is true and correct to the best of my knowledge. I understand that anyone who knowingly gives a false or misleading statement about a material fact in this information, or causes someone else to do so, commits a crime and may be sent to prison, or may face other penalties, or both.

EITHER THE CLAIMANT OR REPRESENTATIVE SHOULD SIGN - ENTER ADDRESSES FOR BOTH

CLAIMANT SIGNATURE — SIGNATURE OR NAME OF CLAIMANT'S REPRESENTATIVE

STREET ADDRESS — REPRESENTATIVE'S ADDRESS

CITY	STATE	ZIP CODE	CITY	STATE	ZIP CODE

TELEPHONE NUMBER — DATE — TELEPHONE NUMBER — DATE

Witnesses are required ONLY if this form has been signed by mark (X). If signed by mark (X), two witnesses to the signing who know the person requesting reconsideration must sign below, giving their full addresses.

1. SIGNATURE OF WITNESS — 2. SIGNATURE OF WITNESS

ADDRESS (NUMBER AND STREET, CITY, STATE, ZIP CODE) ADDRESS (NUMBER AND STREET, CITY, STATE, ZIP CODE)

PRIVACY ACT AND PAPERWORK REDUCTION ACT NOTICE

Sections 205(a), (b), 1631(c)(1)(A) and (B), of the Social Security Act, as amended, allow us to collect this information. We will use the information you provide to determine your eligibility for disability benefits.

Furnishing us this information is voluntary. However, failure to provide us with all or part of the information may prevent us from re-evaluating the decision on your claim.

We rarely use the information you supply for any purpose other than what we state above, however, we may use the information for the administration of our programs including sharing information:

1. To comply with Federal laws requiring the release of information from our record (e.g., to the Government Accountability Office and Department of Veterans Affairs);and,

2. To facilitate statistical research, audit, or investigative activities necessary to ensure the integrity and improvement of our programs (e.g., to the Bureau of the Census and to private entities under contract with us).

A complete list of when we may share your information with others, called routine uses, is available in our Privacy Act System of Records Notices, 60-0009, entitled Hearings and Appeals Case Control System, 60-0010, entitled Hearing Office Tracking System of Claimant Cases, and 60-0089, entitled Claims Folders Systems. Additional information about these and other system of records notices and our programs are available from our Internet website at www.socialsecurity.gov or at your local Social Security office.

We may also use the information you provide in computer matching programs. Matching programs compare our records with records kept by other Federal, State, or local government agencies. Information from these matching programs can be used to establish or verify a person's eligibility for federally-funded or administered benefit programs and for repayment of payments or delinquent debts under these programs.

Paperwork Reduction Act Statement - This information collection meets the requirements of 44 U.S.C. § 3507, as amended by section 2 of the Paperwork Reduction Act of 1995. You do not need to answer these questions unless we display a valid Office of Management and Budget (OMB) control number. The OMB control number for this collection is 0960-0349. We estimate that it will take about 13 minutes to read the instructions, gather the facts, and answer the questions. **SEND OR BRING THE COMPLETED FORM TO YOUR LOCAL SOCIAL SECURITY OFFICE. You can find your local Social Security office through SSA's website at** www.socialsecurity.gov. **Offices are also listed under U. S. Government agencies in your telephone directory or you may call Social Security at 1-800-772-1213 (TTY 1-800-325-0778).** *You may send comments on our time estimate above to: SSA, 6401 Security Blvd, Baltimore, MD 21235-0001. Send only comments relating to our time estimate to this address, not the completed form.*

Disability Report SSA-3441-BK

https://ssa.gov/forms/ssa-3441.pdf

DISABILITY REPORT - APPEAL
SSA-3441-BK

PLEASE READ THIS INFORMATION BEFORE COMPLETING THIS REPORT

This report is used to update your information for your disability appeal. Completing this report accurately helps us process your claim. Please complete as much of this report as you can.

IF YOU NEED HELP

Please do not ask your health care provider to complete this report. You can get help from other people, such as a friend or family member. If you cannot complete this report, a Social Security representative can assist you. If you make an appointment with us, please complete as much of this report as you can and have it with you for your appointment.

HOW TO COMPLETE THIS REPORT

If you have Internet access, you may be able to complete this report online at www.ssa.gov/disability/appeal

If you complete this report on paper:

- Print or write clearly.

- Include a ZIP or postal code with each address.

- Provide complete phone numbers, including area code. If a phone number is outside the United States, also provide International Direct Dialing (IDD) code and country code.

- If you cannot remember the names and addresses of your health care providers, you may be able to get that information from the telephone book, Internet, medical bills, prescriptions, or prescription medicine containers.

- **ANSWER EVERY QUESTION**, unless this report indicates otherwise. You can write "don't know," or "none," or "does not apply" if you need to.

- If you need more space to answer any question, please use the REMARKS section on the last page, SECTION 10. Include the number of the question you are answering.

YOUR MEDICAL RECORDS

If you have any medical records that you have not given to us, send or bring them to our office with this completed report. Please tell us if you want us to return them to you. If you are having an interview in our office, bring your medical records, your prescription medicine containers (if available), and this completed report with you.

YOU DO NOT NEED TO ASK DOCTORS OR HOSPITALS FOR ANY MEDICAL RECORDS THAT YOU DO NOT ALREADY HAVE. With your permission, we will request your records. The information that you give us on this report tells us where to request your medical and other records.

HOW TO SUBMIT THIS REPORT

Send or bring this completed report to your local Social Security office. If you have Internet access, you can locate your nearest Social Security office by zip code at www.socialsecurity.gov/locator. Our offices are also listed under U.S. Government agencies in your telephone directory or you may call Social Security at 1-800-772-1213 (TTY 1-800-325-0778).

~ 134 ~

SOCIAL SECURITY ADMINISTRATION

Form Approved
OMB No. 0960-0144

DISABILITY REPORT – APPEAL

For SSA use only. Please do not write in this box.

Related SSN _____   Number Holder _____

If you are filling out this report for someone else, please provide information about him or her. When a question refers to "you" or "your", it refers to the person who is applying for disability benefits.

SECTION 1 – INFORMATION ABOUT THE DISABLED PERSON

1. A. Name (First, Middle, Last, Suffix)

1. B. Social Security Number

1. C. Daytime Phone Number, including area code (include IDD and country codes if outside the U.S. or Canada)

☐ Check this box if you do not have a phone number where we can leave a message

1. D. Alternate Phone Number – another number where we may reach you, if any

1. E. Email Address (Optional)

SECTION 2 – CONTACTS

Give the name of someone **(other than your doctors)** we can contact who knows about your medical conditions and can help you with your claim (e.g. friend or relative)

2. A. Name (First, Middle, Last)

2. B. Relationship to Disabled Person

2. C. Mailing Address (Street or PO Box), include apartment number or unit if applicable

City	State/Province	ZIP/Postal Code	Country (if not U.S.)

2. D. Daytime Phone Number, including area code (include IDD and country codes if outside the U.S. or Canada)

2. E. Can this person speak and understand English?
☐ Yes   ☐ No

If no, what language does the contact person prefer?

2. F. Who is completing this form?
☐ The person who is applying for disability (Go to SECTION 3 - MEDICAL CONDITIONS).
☐ The person listed in 2 A. (Go to SECTION 3 - MEDICAL CONDITIONS).
☐ Someone else (Please complete the information below).

2. G. Name (First, Middle, Last)

2. H. Relationship to Disabled Person

2. I. Mailing Address (Street or PO Box) Include apartment number or unit if applicable

City	State/Province	ZIP/Postal Code	Country (if not U.S.)

2. J. Daytime Phone Number, including area code (include IDD and country codes if outside the U.S. or Canada)

~ 135 ~

SECTION 3 – MEDICAL CONDITIONS

3. A. Since you last told us about your medical conditions, has there been any **CHANGE** (for better or worse) in your physical or mental conditions?

☐ Yes, approximate date change occurred _____   ☐ No

If yes, please describe in detail _____

_____

_____

3. B. Since you last told us about your medical conditions, do you have any **NEW** physical or mental conditions?

☐ Yes, approximate date of new conditions _____   ☐ No

If yes, please describe in detail _____

_____

_____

If you need more space, use SECTION 10 – REMARKS on the last page.

SECTION 4 – MEDICAL TREATMENT

4. A. Have you used any other names on your medical or educational records? Examples are maiden name, other married name, or nickname

☐ Yes   ☐ No

If yes, please list the other names used _____

4. B. Since you last told us about your medical treatment, have you seen a doctor or other health care provider, received treatment at a hospital or clinic, or **do you have a future appointment scheduled**?

☐ Yes   ☐ No (Go to SECTION 6 – MEDICINES)

4. C. What type(s) of condition(s) were you treated for, or will you be seen for?

☐ Physical   ☐ Mental (including emotional or learning problems)

If you answered "Yes" to 4.B., please tell us who may have **NEW** medical records about any of your **physical or mental** conditions (including emotional or learning problems)

Use the following pages to provide information for up to three (3) providers. **Complete one page for each provider.** If you have more than three providers, list them in SECTION 10 - REMARKS on the last page.

Please include

- doctors' offices
- hospitals (including emergency room visits)
- clinics
- mental health center
- other health care facilities

Only list the providers you have seen since you last told us about your medical treatment.

4. D. Name of facility or office | Name of health care provider who treated you

ALL OF THE QUESTIONS ON THIS PAGE REFER TO THE HEALTH CARE PROVIDER ABOVE.

Phone Number | Patient ID# (if known)

Address

City | State/Province | ZIP/Postal Code | Country (if not U.S.)

Dates of Treatment (approximate date, if exact date is unknown)

Office, Clinic or Outpatient visits at this facility	Emergency Room visits at this facility	Overnight hospital stays at this facility
First Visit _____	Date _____	Date in _____ Date out _____
Last Visit _____	Date _____	Date in _____ Date out _____
Next scheduled appointment	Date _____	Date in _____ Date out _____
(if any) _____	☐ None	☐ None

What medical conditions were treated or evaluated?

What treatment did you receive for the above conditions? (Do not list medicines or tests in this box.)

Has this provider performed or sent you to any tests? Please include tests you are scheduled to have in the future. ☐ Yes (Please complete the information below.) ☐ No (Go to the next page.)

KIND OF TEST	DATES OF TESTS	KIND OF TEST	DATES OF TESTS
Biopsy (list body part)		MRI/CT Scan (list body part)	
Blood Test (not HIV)		Speech/Language Test	
Breathing Test		Treadmill (exercise test)	
Cardiac Catheterization		Vision Test	
EEG (brain wave test)		X-ray (list body part)	
EKG (heart test)			
Hearing Test		Other (please describe)	
HIV Test			
IQ Testing			

If you need to list more tests, use SECTION 10 - REMARKS on the last page

If you do not have any more providers to describe,

go to SECTION 5 – OTHER MEDICAL INFORMATION on page 6.

Form **SSA-3441-BK** (03-2015) ef (03-2015)   Page 3

SECTION 4 – MEDICAL TREATMENT (continued)
Provider 2

4. D. Name of facility or office | Name of health care provider who treated you

ALL OF THE QUESTIONS ON THIS PAGE REFER TO THE HEALTH CARE PROVIDER ABOVE.

Phone Number | Patient ID# (if known)

Address

City | State/Province | ZIP/Postal Code | Country (if not U.S.)

Dates of Treatment (approximate date, if exact date is unknown)

Office, Clinic or Outpatient visits at this facility	Emergency Room visits at this facility	Overnight hospital stays at this facility
First Visit _____	Date _____	Date in _____ Date out _____
Last Visit _____	Date _____	Date in _____ Date out _____
Next scheduled appointment	Date _____	Date in _____ Date out _____
(if any) _____	☐ None	☐ None

What medical conditions were treated or evaluated?

What treatment did you receive for the above conditions? (Do not list medicines or tests in this box.)

Has this provider performed or sent you to any tests? Please include tests you are scheduled to have in the future   ☐ Yes (Please complete the information below.)   ☐ No (Go to the next page.)

KIND OF TEST	DATES OF TESTS	KIND OF TEST	DATES OF TESTS
☐ Biopsy (list body part) _____		☐ MRI/CT Scan (list body part) _____	
☐ Blood Test (not HIV)		☐ Speech/Language Test	
☐ Breathing Test		☐ Treadmill (exercise test)	
☐ Cardiac Cathetenzation		☐ Vision Test	
☐ EEG (brain wave test)		☐ X-ray (list body part) _____	
☐ EKG (heart test)			
☐ Hearing Test		☐ Other (please describe) _____	
☐ HIV Test			
☐ IQ Testing			

If you need to list more tests, use SECTION 10 - REMARKS on the last page.

If you do not have any more providers to describe,
go to SECTION 5 – OTHER MEDICAL INFORMATION on page 6.

Form **SSA-3441-BK** (03-2015) ef (03-2015)   Page 4

~ 138 ~

SECTION 4 – MEDICAL TREATMENT (continued)
Provider 3

4. D. Name of facility or office   Name of health care provider who treated you

ALL OF THE QUESTIONS ON THIS PAGE REFER TO THE HEALTH CARE PROVIDER ABOVE.

Phone Number   Patient ID# (if known)

Address

City   State/Province   ZIP/Postal Code   Country (if not U.S.)

Dates of Treatment (approximate date, if exact date is unknown)

Office, Clinic or Outpatient visits at this facility	Emergency Room visits at this facility	Overnight hospital stays at this facility
First Visit _____	Date _____	Date in _____ Date out _____
Last Visit _____	Date _____	Date in _____ Date out _____
Next scheduled appointment	Date _____	Date in _____ Date out _____
(if any) _____	☐ None	☐ None

What medical conditions were treated or evaluated?

What treatment did you receive for the above conditions? (Do not list medicines or tests in this box.)

Has this provider performed or sent you to any tests? Please include tests you are scheduled to have in the future. ☐ Yes (Please complete the information below.)   ☐ No (Go to the next page.)

KIND OF TEST	DATES OF TESTS	KIND OF TEST	DATES OF TESTS
☐ Biopsy (list body part)		☐ MRI/CT Scan (list body part)	
_____		_____	
☐ Blood Test (not HIV)		☐ Speech/Language Test	
☐ Breathing Test		☐ Treadmill (exercise test)	
☐ Cardiac Catheterization		☐ Vision Test	
☐ EEG (brain wave test)		☐ X-ray (list body part)	
☐ EKG (heart test)		_____	
☐ Hearing Test		☐ Other (please describe)	
☐ HIV Test		_____	
☐ IQ Testing			

If you need to list more tests, use SECTION 10 - REMARKS on the last page.

If you have been treated by more providers, use section 10 - REMARKS on the last page.

Form **SSA-3441-BK** (03-2015) ef (03-2015)   Page 5

~ 139 ~

SECTION 5 – OTHER MEDICAL INFORMATION

5. **Since you last told us about your other medical information**, does anyone else have **medical information** about any of your **physical or mental** conditions (including emotional and learning problems) or are you scheduled to see anyone else?

This may include

- workers' compensation
- vocational rehabilitation services
- insurance companies who have paid you disability benefits
- prisons and correctional facilities
- attorneys
- social service agencies
- welfare agencies
- school/education records

☐ Yes (Please complete the information below.)
☐ No (Go to SECTION 6 – MEDICINES)

Name of Organization	Claim or ID Number (if any)

Address

City	State/Province	ZIP/Postal Code	Country (if not U.S.)

Name of Contact Person	Phone Number

Date of First Contact	Date of Last Contact	Date of Next Contact (if any)

Reasons for Contacts

If you need to list more people or organizations, use SECTION 10 – REMARKS on the last page.

SECTION 6 – MEDICINES

6. Are you currently taking any medicines (prescription or non-prescription)?

☐ Yes (Please complete the information below. You may need to look at your medicine containers.)
☐ No (Go to SECTION 7 – ACTIVITIES)

NAME OF MEDICINE	IF PRESCRIBED, NAME OF DOCTOR	REASON FOR MEDICINE	SIDE EFFECTS YOU HAVE

If you need to list more medicines, use SECTION 10 – REMARKS on the last page.

SECTION 7 - ACTIVITIES

7. Since you last told us about your activities, has there been any **change** (for better or worse) in your daily activities due to your **physical or mental** conditions? (Examples of daily activities are household tasks, personal care, getting around, hobbies and interests, social activities, etc.)

☐ Yes ☐ No

If yes, please describe in detail:

_____

_____

_____

If you need more space, use SECTION 10 – REMARKS on the last page.

SECTION 8 – WORK AND EDUCATION

8. A. Since you last told us about your work, have you worked or has your work changed?

☐ Yes ☐ No

If yes, you will be asked to provide additional information.

8. B. Since you last told us about your education, have you completed or are you enrolled in any type of specialized job training, trade school, or vocational school?

☐ Yes ☐ No

If yes, what type? _____

Date(s) attended _____

If you need more space, use SECTION 10 – REMARKS on the last page.

SECTION 9 – VOCATIONAL REHABILITATION, EMPLOYMENT, OR OTHER SUPPORT SERVICES

9. Since you last told us about your vocational rehabilitation, have you participated, or are you participating in

- an individual work plan with an employment network under the Ticket to Work Program?
- an individualized plan for employment with a vocational rehabilitation agency or any other organization?
- a Plan to Achieve Self-Support (PASS)?
- an individualized education program (IEP) through an educational institution (if a student age 18-21)?
- any program providing vocational rehabilitation, employment services, or other support services to help you go to work?

☐ Yes (Please complete the information below.)
☐ No (Go to SECTION 10 – REMARKS)

Name of Organization or School

_____

Name of Counselor, Instructor, or Job Coach   Phone Number

_____

Address

_____

City   State/Province   ZIP/Postal Code   Country (if not U.S.)

_____

Date when you started participating in the plan or program

If you need more space, use SECTION 10 – REMARKS on the last page.

Form **SSA-3441-BK** (03-2015) ef (03-2015)   Page 7

~ 141 ~

SECTION 10 – REMARKS

Use this space to provide any information you could not show in earlier sections of this form or any additional information you feel we should know about. Please be sure to include the number of the question you are answering. (For example, 3A, 4D, etc.)

Date Report Completed MM/DD/YYYY

Benefit Continuation Election Statement
SSA Form 795

https://www.ssa.gov/forms/ssa-795.pdf

Social Security Administration

Form Approved
OMB No. 0960-0045

STATEMENT OF CLAIMANT OR OTHER PERSON

Name of Wage Earner, Self-employed Person, or SSI Claimant	Social Security Number
Name of Person Making Statement *(If other than above wage earner, self-employed person, or SSI claimant)*	Relationship to Wage Earner, Self-Employed Person, or SSI Claimant

Understanding that this statement is for the use of the Social Security Administration, I hereby certify that -

~ 143 ~

I declare under penalty of perjury that I have examined all the information on this form, and on any accompanying statements or forms, and it is true and correct to the best of my knowledge. I understand that anyone who knowingly gives a false statement about a material fact in this information, or causes someone else to do so, commits a crime and may be subject to a fine or imprisonment.

SIGNATURE OF PERSON MAKING STATEMENT

Signature (First name, middle initial, last name) (Write in ink)	Date (Month, day, year)
	Telephone Number (Include Area Code)

Mailing Address (Number and street, Apt. No.,P.O.Box, Rural Route)

City and State	ZIP Code

Witnesses are required ONLY if this statement has been signed by mark (X) above. If signed by mark (X), two witnesses to the signing who know the individual must sign below, giving their full addresses.

1. Signature of Witness	2. Signature of Witness
Address (Number and street, City, State, and ZIP Code)	Address (Number and street, City, State, and ZIP Code)

Privacy Act Statement
Collection and Use of Personal Information

Section 205a of the Social Security Act (42 U.S.C. § 405a), as amended, authorizes us to collect the information on this form. We will use this information to determine your potential eligibility for benefit payments.

Furnishing us this information is voluntary. However, failing to provide us with all or part of the requested information may affect our ability to evaluate the decision on your claim.

We rarely use the information you provide for any purpose other than for determining entitlement to benefit payments. However, we may use the information you give us for the administration and integrity of our programs. We may also disclose information to another person or to another agency in accordance with approved routine uses, which include, but are not limited to, the following:

1. To enable a third party or an agency to assist us in establishing rights to Social Security benefits and/or coverage;
2. To comply with Federal laws requiring the release of information from our records (e.g., to the Government Accountability Office and the Department of Veterans' Affairs);
3. To make determinations for eligibility in similar health and income maintenance programs at the Federal, State, and local level; and,
4. To facilitate statistical research, audit, or investigative activities necessary to assure the integrity and improvement of Social Security programs.

We may also use the information you provide in computer matching programs. Matching programs compare our records with records kept by other Federal, State, or local government agencies. We use the information from these programs to establish or verify a person's eligibility for federally-funded or administered benefit programs and for repayment or incorrect payments or delinquent debts under these programs.

A complete list of routine uses for this information is available in our Privacy Act Systems of Records Notices, 60-0089, Claims Folders Systems. This notice and additional information regarding our programs and systems are available online at www.socialsecurity.gov or at your local Social Security office.

Paperwork Reduction Act Statement - This information collection meets the requirements of 44 U.S.C. §3507, as amended by Section 2 of the Paperwork Reduction Act of 1995. You do not need to answer these questions unless we display a valid Office of Management and Budget control number. We estimate that it will take about 15 minutes to read the instructions, gather the facts, and answer the questions **SEND THE COMPLETED FORM TO YOUR LOCAL SOCIAL SECURITY OFFICE. The office is listed under U. S. Government agencies in your telephone directory or you may call Social Security at 1-800-772-1213 (TTY 1-800-325-0778).** You may send comments on our time estimate above to: SSA, 6401 Security Boulevard, Baltimore, MD 21235-6401. **Send only comments relating to our time estimate to this address, not the completed form.**

Form **SSA-795** (09-2015) ef (09-2015)

~ 144 ~

Request for Hearing
by Administrative Law Judge
HA-501-U5

https://www.ssa.gov/forms/ha-501.html

SOCIAL SECURITY ADMINISTRATION
OFFICE OF DISABILITY ADJUDICATION AND REVIEW

Form Approved
OMB No. 0960-0269

REQUEST FOR HEARING BY ADMINISTRATIVE LAW JUDGE

See Privacy
Act Notice

*(Take or mail the **completed original** to your local Social Security office, the Veterans Affairs Regional Office in Manila or any U.S. Foreign Service post and keep a copy for your records)*

1. Claimant Name   2. Claimant SSN   3. Claim Number if different

4. I REQUEST A HEARING BEFORE AN ADMINISTRATIVE LAW JUDGE. I disagree with the determination because

An Administrative Law Judge of the Social Security Administration's Office of Disability Adjudication and Review or the Department of Health and Human Services will be appointed to conduct the hearing or other proceedings in your case. You will receive notice of the time and place of a hearing at least 20 days before the date set for a hearing.

5. I have additional evidence to submit. ☐ Yes ☐ No

Name and source of additional evidence, if not included

Submit your evidence to the hearing office within 10 days. Your servicing Social Security office will provide the hearing office's address. Attach an additional sheet if you need more space.

6. Do not complete if the appeal is a Medicare issue. Otherwise, check one of the blocks

☐ I wish to appear at a hearing

☐ I do not wish to appear at a hearing and I request that a decision be made based on the evidence in my case. (Complete Waiver Form HA-4608)

Representation: You have a right to be represented at the hearing. If you are not represented, your Social Security office will give you a list of legal referral and service organizations. If you are represented, complete and submit form SSA-1696 (Appointment of Representative) unless you are appealing a Medicare issue.

7. CLAIMANT SIGNATURE (OPTIONAL)   DATE   8. NAME OF REPRESENTATIVE (if any)   DATE

RESIDENCE ADDRESS   ADDRESS

CITY   STATE   ZIP CODE   CITY   STATE   ZIP CODE

TELEPHONE NUMBER   FAX NUMBER   TELEPHONE NUMBER   FAX NUMBER

TO BE COMPLETED BY SOCIAL SECURITY ADMINISTRATION- ACKNOWLEDGMENT OF REQUEST FOR HEARING

9. Request received on _____ by _____
      (Date)   (Print Name)   (Title)

(Address)   (Servicing FO Code)   (PC Code)

10. Was the request for hearing received within 65 days of the reconsidered determination? ☐ Yes ☐ No
If no, attach claimant's explanation for delay and supporting documents if any.

11. If claimant is not represented, was a list of legal referral service organizations provided? ☐ Yes ☐ No

12. Interpreter needed ☐ Yes ☐ No
Language (including sign language)

13. Check one ☐ Initial Entitlement Case
☐ Disability Cessation Case or ☐ Other Postentitlement Case

14. HO COPY SENT TO _____ HO on _____
☐ Claims Folder (CF) Attached ☐ Title (T) II ☐ T XVI
☐ T VIII, ☐ T XVIII, ☐ T II CF held in FO ☐ Electronic Folder
☐ CF requested ☐ T II ☐ T XVI ☐ T VIII ☐ T XVIII
(Copy of email or phone report attached)

16. CF COPY SENT TO _____ HO on _____
☐ CF Attached ☐ Title (T) II ☐ T XVI ☐ T XVIII
☐ Other Attached

15. Check all claim types that apply
☐ Retirement and Survivors Insurance Only   (RSI)
☐ Title II Disability - Worker or child only   (DIWC)
☐ Title II Disability - Widow(er) only   (DIWW)
☐ Title XVI (SSI) Aged only   (SSIA)
☐ Title XVI Blind only   (SSIB)
☐ Title XVI Disability only   (SSID)
☐ Title XVI/Title II Concurrent Aged Claim   (SSAC)
☐ Title XVI/Title II Concurrent Blind   (SSBC)
☐ Title XVI/Title II Concurrent Disability   (SSDC)
☐ Title XVIII Hospital/Supplementary Insurance   (HI/SMI)
☐ Title VIII Only Special Veterans Benefits   (SVB)
☐ Title VIII/Title XVI   (SVB/SSI)
☐ Other - Specify

Form **HA-501-U5** (01-2015) ef (01-2015)
Use 08-2012 Edition Until Stock is Exhausted

TAKE OR SEND ORIGINAL TO SSA AND RETAIN A COPY FOR YOUR RECORDS

~ 146 ~

Medical Release Form SSA-827

https://www.ssa.gov/forms/ssa-827.pdf

WHOSE *Records to be Disclosed*	Form Approved OMB No. 0960-0623
NAME *(First, Middle, Last, Suffix)*	
SSN	Birthday *(mm/dd/yy)*

AUTHORIZATION TO DISCLOSE INFORMATION TO THE SOCIAL SECURITY ADMINISTRATION (SSA)
** PLEASE READ THE ENTIRE FORM, BOTH PAGES, BEFORE SIGNING BELOW **

I voluntarily authorize and request disclosure (including paper, oral, and electronic interchange):
OF WHAT *All my medical records; also education records and other information related to my ability to perform tasks. This includes specific permission to release:*

1. All records and other information regarding my treatment, hospitalization, and outpatient care for my impairment(s) *including*, and not limited to:
   - Psychological, psychiatric or other mental impairment(s) (excludes "psychotherapy notes" as defined in 45 CFR 164.501)
   - Drug abuse, alcoholism, or other substance abuse
   - Sickle cell anemia
   - Records which may indicate the presence of a communicable or noncommunicable disease, and tests for or records of HIV/AIDS
   - Gene-related impairments (including genetic test results)
2. Information about how my impairment(s) affects my ability to complete tasks and activities of daily living, and affects my ability to work.
3. Copies of educational tests or evaluations, including Individualized Educational Programs, triennial assessments, psychological and speech evaluations, and any other records that can help evaluate function; also teachers' observations and evaluations.
4. Information created within 12 months after the date this authorization is signed, as well as past information.

FROM WHOM

- All medical sources (hospitals, clinics, labs, physicians, psychologists, etc.) including mental health, correctional, addiction treatment, and VA health care facilities
- All educational sources (schools, teachers, records administrators, counselors, etc.)
- Social workers/rehabilitation counselors
- Consulting examiners used by SSA
- Employers, insurance companies, workers' compensation programs
- Others who may know about my condition (family, neighbors, friends, public officials)

THIS BOX TO BE COMPLETED BY SSA/DDS (as needed) Additional information to identify the subject (e.g., other names used), the specific source, or the material to be disclosed.

TO WHOM The Social Security Administration and to the State agency authorized to process my case (usually called "disability determination services") including contract copy services, and doctors or other professionals consulted during the process. [Also, for international claims, to the U.S. Department of State Foreign Service Post.]

PURPOSE Determining my eligibility for benefits, including looking at the combined effect of any impairments that by themselves would not meet SSA's definition of disability, and whether I can manage such benefits
☐ Determining whether I am capable of managing benefits ONLY (check only if this applies)

EXPIRES WHEN This authorization is good for 12 months from the date signed (below my signature)

- I authorize the use of a copy (including electronic copy) of this form for the disclosure of the information described above.
- I understand that there are some circumstances in which this information may be redisclosed to other parties (see page 2 for details).
- I may write to SSA and my sources to revoke this authorization at any time (see page 2 for details).
- SSA will give me a copy of this form if I ask. I may ask the source to allow me to inspect or get a copy of material to be disclosed.
- I have read both pages of this form and agree to the disclosures above from the types of sources listed.

PLEASE SIGN USING BLUE OR BLACK INK ONLY	IF not signed by subject of disclosure, specify basis for authority to sign
INDIVIDUAL authorizing disclosure	☐ Parent of minor ☐ Guardian ☐ Other personal representative (explain)
SIGN ▶	(Parent/guardian/personal representative sign here if two signatures required by State law) ▶
Date Signed	Street Address
Phone Number (with area code)	City	State	ZIP

WITNESS *I know the person signing this form or am satisfied of this person's identity:*

SIGN ▶	SIGN ▶ (If needed, second witness sign here (e.g., if signed with "X" above))
Phone Number (or Address)	Phone Number (or Address)

This general and special authorization to disclose was developed to comply with the provisions regarding disclosure of medical, educational, and other information under P.L. 104-191 ("HIPAA"), 45 CFR parts 160 and 164; 42 U.S. Code section 290dd-2; 42 CFR part 2; 38 U.S. Code section 7332; 38 CFR 1.475; 20 U.S. Code section 1232g ("FERPA"); 34 CFR parts 99 and 300; and State law.
Form SSA-827 (11-2012) ef (11-2012) Use 4-2009 and Later Editions Until Supply is Exhausted   Page 1 of 2

Explanation of Form SSA-827,
"Authorization to Disclose Information to the Social Security Administration (SSA)"

We need your written authorization to help get the information required to process your claim, and to determine your capability of managing benefits. Laws and regulations require that sources of personal information have a signed authorization before releasing it to us. Also, laws require specific authorization for the release of information about certain conditions and from educational sources.

You can provide this authorization by signing a form SSA-827. Federal law permits sources with information about you to release that information if you sign a single authorization to release all your information from all your possible sources. We will make copies of it for each source. A covered entity (that is, a source of medical information about you) may not condition treatment, payment, enrollment, or eligibility for benefits on whether you sign this authorization form. A few States, and some individual sources of information, require that the authorization specifically name the source that you authorize to release personal information. In those cases, we may ask you to sign one authorization for each source and we may contact you again if we need you to sign more authorizations.

You have the right to revoke this authorization at any time, except to the extent a source of information has already relied on it to take an action. To revoke, send a written statement to any Social Security Office. If you do, also send a copy directly to any of your sources that you no longer wish to disclose information about you. SSA can tell you if we identified any sources you didn't tell us about. SSA may use information disclosed prior to revocation to decide your claim.

It is SSA's policy to provide service to people with limited English proficiency in their native language or preferred mode of communication consistent with Executive Order 13166 (August 11, 2000) and the Individuals with Disabilities Education Act. SSA makes every reasonable effort to ensure that the information in the SSA-827 is provided to you in your native or preferred language.

Privacy Act Statement
Collection and Use of Personal Information

Sections 205(a), 233(d)(5)(A), 1614(a)(3)(H)(i), 1631(d)(1) and 1631(e)(1)(A) of the Social Security Act as amended, [42 U.S.C. 405(a), 433(d)(5)(A), 1382c(a)(3)(H)(i), 1383(d)(1) and 1383(e)(1)(A)] authorize us to collect this information. We will use the information you provide to help us determine your eligibility, or continuing eligibility for benefits, and your ability to manage any benefits received. The information you provide is voluntary. However, failure to provide the requested information may prevent us from making an accurate and timely decision on your claim, and could result in denial or loss of benefits.

We rarely use the information you provide on this form for any purpose other than for the reasons explained above. However, we may use it for the administration and integrity of Social Security programs. We may also disclose information to another person or to another agency in accordance with approved routine uses, including but not limited to the following:

1. To enable a third party or an agency to assist us in establishing rights to Social Security benefits and/or coverage;

2. To comply with Federal laws requiring the release of information from our records (e.g., to the Government Accountability Office, General Services Administration, National Archives Records Administration, and the Department of Veterans Affairs);

3. To make determinations for eligibility in similar health and income maintenance programs at the Federal, State, and local level; and

4. To facilitate statistical research, audit, or investigative activities necessary to assure the integrity and improvement of our programs (e.g., to the U.S. Census Bureau and to private entities under contract with us).

We may also use the information you provide in computer matching programs. Matching programs compare our records with records kept by other Federal, State, or local government agencies. We use the information from these programs to establish or verify a person's eligibility for Federally funded or administered benefit programs and for repayment of incorrect payments or delinquent debts under these programs.

A complete list of routine uses of the information you gave us is available in our Privacy Act Systems of Records Notices entitled, Claims Folder System, 60-0089, Master Beneficiary Record, 60-0090; Supplemental Security Income record and Special Veterans benefits, 60-0103, and Electronic Disability (eDIB) Claims File, 60-0340. The notices, additional information regarding this form, and information regarding our systems and programs, are available on-line at www.socialsecurity.gov or at any Social Security office.

Paperwork Reduction Act Statement - This information collection meets the requirements of 44 U.S.C. § 3507, as amended by section 2 of the Paperwork Reduction Act of 1995. You do not need to answer these questions unless we display a valid Office of Management and Budget control number. We estimate that it will take about 10 minutes to read the instructions, gather the facts, and answer the questions. **SEND OR BRING THE COMPLETED FORM TO YOUR LOCAL SOCIAL SECURITY OFFICE.** You can find your local Social Security office through SSA's website at www.socialsecurity.gov. Offices are also listed under U.S. Government agencies in your telephone directory or you may call Social Security at 1-800-772-1213 (TTY 1-800-325-0778). *You may send comments on our time estimate above to: SSA, 6401 Security Blvd, Baltimore, MD 21235-6401. Send only comments relating to our time estimate to this address, not the completed form.*

COMPASSIONATE ALLOWANCES

We have provided a list of Compassionate Allowances. Title XVI of the Social Security Act authorizes SSI benefits. The Compassionate Allowances (CAL) initiative is a way to expedite the processing of SSDI and SSI disability claims for applicants whose medical conditions are so severe that their conditions obviously meet Social Security's definition of disability. If you originally had your claim allowed under this section of the law, make sure that Social Security remembers that. Also, if your condition has gotten worse over time, you may want to review the list to see if you now qualify.

**Social Security Disability
Compassionate Allowance Conditions**

1. Acute Leukemia
2. Adrenal Cancer - with distant metastases or inoperable, unresectable or recurrent
3. Alexander Disease (ALX) - Neonatal and Infantile
4. Alstrom Syndrome
5. Amegakaryocytic Thrombocytopenia
6. Amyotrophic Lateral Sclerosis (ALS)
7. Anaplastic Adrenal Cancer - with distant metastases or inoperable, unresectable or recurrent
8. Astrocytoma - Grade III and IV
9. Ataxia Spinocerebellar

10. Ataxia Telangiectasia
11. Batten Disease
12. Bilateral Retinoblastoma
13. Bladder Cancer - with distant metastases or inoperable or unresectable
14. Bone Cancer - with distant metastases or inoperable or unresectable
15. Breast Cancer - with distant metastases or inoperable or unresectable
16. Canavan Disease (CD)
17. Cerebro Oculo Facio Skeletal (COFS) Syndrome
18. Chronic Myelogenous Leukemia (CML) - Blast Phase
19. Creutzfeldt-Jakob Disease (CJD) - Adult
20. Cri du Chat Syndrome
21. Degos Disease
22. Early-Onset Alzheimer's Disease
23. Edwards Syndrome
24. Ependymoblastoma (Child Brain Tumor)
25. Esophageal Cancer
26. Farber's Disease (FD) - Infantile
27. Fibrodysplasia Ossificans Progressiva
28. Friedreichs Ataxia (FRDA)
29. Frontotemporal Dementia (FTD), Picks Disease -Type A - Adult
30. Fukuyama Congenital Muscular Dystrophy
31. Gallbladder Cancer
32. Gaucher Disease (GD) - Type 2
33. Glioblastoma Multiforme (Brain Tumor)
34. Glutaric Acidemia Type II
35. Head and Neck Cancers - with distant metastasis or inoperable or unresectable
36. Hemophagocytic Lymphohistiocytosis (HLH), Familial Type
37. Hurler Syndrome, Type IH

38.Hunter Syndrome, Type II
39.Idiopathic Pulmonary Fibrosis
40.Inflammatory Breast Cancer (IBC)
41.Junctional Epidermolysis Bullosa, Lethal Type
42.Kidney Cancer - inoperable or unresectable
43.Krabbe Disease (KD) - Infant
44.Large Intestine Cancer - with distant metastasis or inoperable, unresectable or recurrent
45.Late Infantile Neuronal Ceroid Lipofuscinoses
46.Leigh's Disease
47.Liver Cancer
48.Maple Syrup Urine Disease
49.Mantle Cell Lymphoma (MCL)
50.Merosin Deficient Congenital Muscular Dystrophy
51.Metachromatic Leukodystrophy (MLD) - Late Infantile
52.Mixed Dementia
53.Mucosal Malignant Melanoma
54.Niemann-Pick Disease (NPD) - Type A
55.Neonatal Adrenoleukodystrophy
56.Neuronal Ceroid Lipofuscinoses, Infantile Type
57.Niemann-Pick Type C
58.Non-Small Cell Lung Cancer - with metastases to or beyond the hilar nodes or inoperable, unresectable or recurrent
59.Ornithine Transcarbamylase (OTC) Deficiency
60.Osteogenesis Imperfecta (OI) - Type II
61.Ovarian Cancer - with distant metastases or inoperable or unresectable
62.Pancreatic Cancer
63.Patau Syndrome
64.Peritoneal Mesothelioma
65.Pleural Mesothelioma
66.Pompe Disease - Infantile
67.Primary Progressive Aphasia

68.Progressive Multifocal Leukoencephalopathy
69.Rett (RTT) Syndrome
70.Salivary Tumors
71.Sandhoff Disease
72.Sanfilippo Syndrome
73.Small Cell Cancer (of the Large Intestine, Ovary, Prostate, or Uterus)
74.Small Cell Lung Cancer
75.Small Intestine Cancer - with distant metastases or inoperable, unresectable or recurrent
76.Spinal Muscular Atrophy (SMA) - Types 0 And 1
77.Stomach Cancer - with distant metastases or inoperable, unresectable or recurrent
78.Subacute Sclerosis Panencephalitis
79.Tay Sachs Disease
80.Thanatophoric Dysplasia, Type 1
81.Thyroid Cancer
82.Ullrich Congenital Muscular Dystrophy
83.Ureter Cancer - with distant metastases or inoperable, unresectable or recurrent
84.Walker Warburg Syndrome
85.Wolman Disease
86.Zellweger Syndrome

GLOSSARY OF TERMS

Americans with Disabilities Act of 1990 (ADA): Public Law 101-336 gives civil rights protections to individuals with disabilities similar to those provided to individuals on the basis of race, color, sex, national origin, age, and religion. It guarantees equal opportunity for individuals with disabilities in public accommodations, employment, transportation, State and local government services, and telecommunications.

Area Work Incentives Coordinator (AWIC): The AWIC is a Social Security Administration employee who serves as an expert on SSA's work incentives and employment support programs in a specific geographic area of the country. He/she manages and coordinates work incentive training; conducts public outreach; and provides public support services to beneficiaries with disabilities who want to start or keep working and to other members of the community.

Beneficiary: An individual who receives either Social Security Disability Insurance (SSDI) or Supplemental Security Income (SSI) benefits from the Social Security Administration (SSA).

Benefits Planning Query (BPQY): The BPQY is a planning tool that can be used by Area Work Incentives Coordinators, Plan for Achieving Self Support (PASS) Cadre employees and Work Incentive Planning and Assistance (WIPA) projects to provide customized employment services to beneficiaries with disabilities who want to start or keep working. A BPQY provides a snapshot of a beneficiary's current status as

Blind Work expenses (BWE) (SSI): If you are blind, we do not count any earned income that you use to meet expenses in earning that income when we decide your SSI eligibility and payment amount. For example, BWEs include: transportation to and from work, income taxes, attendant care services, and service animal expenses.

Break-Even Point (SSI): The dollar amount of total income that will (after applicable deductions are applied) reduce the SSI payment to zero in a given set of case facts. Your break-even point depends on your earned and unearned income, living arrangements, applicable income exclusions, and state supplement, if any. While useful for discussion purposes, this term does not appear in the SSI rules.

Centers for Medicare and Medicaid Services (CMS): The U.S. Department of Health and Human Services Centers for Medicare and Medicaid Services administers Medicare, Medicaid, and the State Children's Health Insurance Program.

Deeming (SSI): Our process of considering some of the income and resources of your parent, or spouse, or sponsor (if you are an alien) to be your income and resources when you are applying for or receiving SSI benefits.

Definition of Disability (SSDI and SSI): The inability to engage in any substantial gainful activity because of a medically determinable physical or mental impairment(s)

which has lasted or can be expected to last for at least 12 months or can be expected to result in death.

Earned Income Tax Credit (EITC): This is a refundable federal income tax credit for low-income working individuals and families. Congress originally approved the tax credit legislation in 1975 in part to offset the burden of Social Security taxes and to provide an incentive to work. To qualify, taxpayers must meet certain requirements and file a tax return, even if they did not earn enough money to be obligated to file a tax return.

Employment Network (EN): A qualified public or private organization that has entered into a contract with SSA to function as an employment network under the Ticket to Work program and assume responsibility for the coordination and delivery of employment services, vocational rehabilitation services, or other support services to beneficiaries who have assigned their Tickets to that employment network.

Employment Plan: An individual work plan under which an employment network (other than a State vocational rehabilitation agency) provides services to a Social Security Disability Insurance or Supplemental Security Income beneficiary with a disability under the Ticket to Work program, or an individualized plan for employment under which a State Vocational Rehabilitation agency provides services.

Employment Supports (Also known as work incentives): Congress developed employment supports to give individuals with disabilities assistance to move from benefit dependence to independence.

Equal Employment Opportunity Commission (EEOC): The Commission promotes equality of opportunity in the workplace and enforces federal laws prohibiting employment discrimination.

Expedited Reinstatement: A qualified individual may request reinstatement of benefits, within 5 years of benefits having stopped, without having to file a new application. Up to 6 months of provisional benefits are available while we make a decision on the request.

Extended Period of Eligibility: (SSDI) During the 36 consecutive months following the trial work period, if you qualify, we may restart your SSDI benefits without a new application, disability determination, or waiting period.

Impairment-Related Work Expenses (IRWE) (SSDI and SSI): We deduct the cost of items and services that you need to work because of your impairment (e.g., attendant care services, medical devices, etc.) when we decide if you are engaging in substantial gainful activity. It does not matter if you also need the items for normal daily activities. We can usually deduct the cost of these same items from earned income to figure your SSI payment.

Income (SSI) SSI income includes:
•Earned income - money received from wages, including from a sheltered workshop or work activity center, self-employment earnings, and some royalties and honoraria; and
•Unearned income - money received from all other sources, e.g., gifts, interest, Social Security benefits, Veterans benefits, and pensions. Unearned Income also includes "in-kind income" (free food, clothing or shelter) and "deemed

income" (some of the income of a spouse, or parent, or sponsor of an alien).

Income Exclusions (SSI): Generally, if the item received cannot be used as, or to obtain, food, clothing, or shelter, we do not consider it as income. Income exclusions are used to determine countable income. Earned income exclusions include:
•The first $65 per month plus one-half of the remaining earnings;
•Impairment-related work expenses or blind work expenses;
•Income you set aside or use to pursue a Plan for Achieving Self-Support.
Unearned income exclusions include:
•The first $20 per month;
•Income you set aside or use to pursue a Plan for Achieving Self-Support;
•State or locally funded assistance based on need;
•Rent subsidies under HUD programs and the value of food stamps;
•Infrequent or irregularly received income ($20 or less a month).
General earned income exclusion;
•The first $65 ($85 if you have no income other than earnings) of any monthly earned income plus one-half of remaining earnings.

Individual Employment Plan (IEP): An intensive service provided through the one-stop delivery system.
Development of a plan to identify the employment goals, appropriate achievement objectives, and appropriate combination of services for the participant to achieve the employment goals.

Individualized Plan for Employment (IPE): A written plan of action which outlines the employment goal, criteria to evaluate progress toward the employment goal and the services to be provided. It is developed for each individual who is determined to be eligible for vocational rehabilitation services through the state Vocational Rehabilitation (VR) agency. Contact your state VR agency for more information.

Individual Work Plan (IWP): A required written document signed by an Employment Network (EN) (other than a State Vocational Rehabilitation agency) and a beneficiary, or a representative of a beneficiary, with a Ticket to outline the specific employment services, vocational rehabilitation services and other support services that the EN and beneficiary have determined are necessary to achieve the beneficiary's stated employment goal.

Medicaid (Medi-Cal in California, AHCCS in Arizona) (SSI): Medical coverage provided to a person by the State title XIX program.

Medicaid Protection for People with Disabilities Who Work (SSI): For people with disabilities who: have earnings that are too high to qualify for Medicaid under current rules: are at least 16, but less than 65 years of age, and meet state resource and income limits, a state may provide Medicaid coverage. A state may also provide Medicaid coverage to these individuals when they lose coverage due to medical improvement, but still have a medically determinable severe impairment.

Medicaid While Working [Section 1619(b)] (SSI): This is an employment support that is different than Medicaid

Protection for People with Disabilities Who Work. Here your Medicaid coverage can continue, even if your earnings alone or in combination with your other income become too high for a SSI cash payment. To qualify you must have been eligible for a SSI cash payment for at least 1 month; still be disabled; still meet all other eligibility rules, including resource test; need Medicaid in order to work and have gross earned income that is insufficient to replace SSI, Medicaid and any publicly funded attendant care.

Medicare (SSDI): Health insurance program for eligible disabled individuals and individuals age 65 or older usually consisting of:

•Hospital Insurance under Medicare (Part A);
•Supplementary Medical Insurance under Medicare (Part B); and
•Voluntary prescription drug coverage with a Prescription Drug Provider (PDP) under Part D.
Low-income beneficiaries with Medicare can get extra help paying their prescription drug coverage premiums by filing an application with SSA.

Medicare for People with Disabilities Who Work (SSDI) Some people with disabilities who have returned to work can buy continued Medicare coverage when their premium-free Medicare ends due to work activity. States are required to help pay the hospital insurance premiums for some working individuals with disabilities.

Medical Improvement Expected (MIE): When we decide you have a disabling impairment, and we also decide that the disabling impairment(s) may improve, we document that your case will need a future review.

Medicaid Infrastructure Grants (MIG): Section 203 of the Ticket to Work and Work Incentives Improvement Act of 1999 establishes a grant program to support state efforts to enhance employment options for people with disabilities. CMS is the designated agency with administrative responsibility for this grant program.

Medical Improvement Not Expected (MINE): When we decide you have a disabling impairment and also decide the disabling impairment(s) will not improve.

Medical Improvement Possible (MIP): When we decide you have a disabling impairment and also decide that the disabling impairment(s) may improve.

Office of Disability Employment Policy (ODEP): The U.S. Department of Labor's Office of Disability Employment Policy provides national leadership by developing and influencing disability-related employment policy and practice affecting the employment of people with disabilities.

Outcome-Milestone Payment System: The system providing a schedule of payments under the Ticket to Work program to an employment network that includes, in addition to payments during the outcome payment period, payment for completion by a beneficiary of milestones directed toward the goal of permanent employment.

Outcome Payment System: The system providing payments under the Ticket to Work program to an employment network for each month, up to a total of 60 months, during which Social Security disability benefits and Federal SSI cash benefits are not payable to a beneficiary because of the performance of substantial gainful activity (SGA) or by reason of earnings from work. **Plan for Achieving Self-Support (PASS)**: Under an approved PASS, you may set aside income and/or resources over a reasonable time which will enable you to reach a work goal to become financially self-supporting. You then can use the income and resources that you set aside to obtain occupational training or education, purchase occupational equipment, establish a business, etc. We do not count the income and resources that you set aside under a PASS when we decide SSI eligibility and payment amount.

PASS Cadre: SSA employees who are specially trained to assist people when developing a Plan to Achieve Self-Support. PASS experts are located across the country, with at least 1 cadre in each of the 10 SSA regions.
Property Essential for Self-Support (PESS): We do not count some or all of certain property necessary for self-support when we apply the SSI resources test. For example, SSA does not count property such as tools or equipment that are used for work. Or, if an individual has a trade or business, SSA does not count property such as inventory.

Protection and Advocacy for Beneficiaries of Social Security (PABSS): An organization in the private or public sector that has entered into a contract to assist SSA in administering the Ticket to Work program.
Protection and Advocacy for Beneficiaries of Social Security (PABSS) Program: The Social Security Administration, as authorized by the Ticket to Work and

Work Incentives Improvement Act of 1999, awarded Work Assistance Program grants to the designated Protection and Advocacy (P&A) system in each of the 50 States, the District of Columbia, the U.S. Territories of American Samoa, Guam, Northern Mariana Islands, Puerto Rico, the Virgin Islands, and the P&A system for Native Americans. SSA's P&A Program, known as Protection and Advocacy for Beneficiaries of Social Security (PABSS), was created to serve SSDI and SSI beneficiaries who want to work despite their continuing disabilities. PABSS grantees will:

•Assist beneficiaries with disabilities in obtaining information and advice about receiving vocational rehabilitation and employment services.
•Provide advocacy or other related services that beneficiaries with disabilities may need to secure or regain gainful employment.

Red Book: A general reference source about SSDI and SSI employment supports. Published by the Social Security Administration, its purpose is to give a working knowledge of technical provisions so that rehabilitation professionals, advocates and counselors can appropriately advise individuals with disabilities who express an interest in starting or returning to work.

Resources (SSI): Resources are anything you own, such as a bank account, stocks, business assets, real property, or personal property that you can use for your support and maintenance. We do not count all your resources when we determine your SSI eligibility.

Substance Abuse and Mental Health Services Administration (SAMHSA): Within the U.S. Department of Health and Human Services, whose mission it is to focus on building resilience and facilitating recovery for people with, or at risk for, mental or substance use disorders.

Substantial Gainful Activity (SGA): We evaluate the work activity of persons claiming or receiving disability benefits under SSDI, and/or claiming benefits because of a disability (other than blindness) under SSI. Under both programs, we use earnings guidelines to evaluate your work activity to decide whether the work activity is substantial gainful activity and whether we may consider you disabled under the law. While this is only one of the tests used to decide if you are disabled, it is a critical first step in a disability evaluation. (For SGA amounts, visit SGA Page.)

Social Security Disability Insurance (SSDI): Social Security Disability Insurance authorized under title II of the Social Security Act.

Supplemental Security Income (SSI): Supplemental Security Income program authorized under title XVI of the Social Security Act.

State Vocational Rehabilitation Agency (State VR agency): The organization in each State, the District of Columbia or U.S. Territory, that is the designated governmental entity responsible for providing vocational rehabilitation services to persons with disabilities residing within its jurisdiction. In some States a separate State Vocational Rehabilitation agency also exists to provide assistance and services to individuals with a visual impairment.

Subsidies and Special Conditions (SSDI and SSI): Supports you receive on the job that may result in more pay than the actual value of the work you perform. We use only the actual value of the work you perform when we make a SGA decision.

Ticket Under the Ticket to Work Program ("Ticket"): A document which provides evidence of the Commissioner's agreement to pay an employment network or a State vocational rehabilitation agency, to which a disabled beneficiary's Ticket is assigned, for providing employment services, vocational rehabilitation services, and other support services to the beneficiary.

Ticket to Work Program: The Ticket to Work Program is a voluntary program that offers SSDI and SSI beneficiaries with disabilities a variety of choices in obtaining the support and services they need to help them go to work and achieve their employment goals. If you are eligible and would like to work or increase your current earnings, this program can help you get vocational rehabilitation, training, job referrals, and other ongoing support and services to help you do so.

Timely Progress: The guidelines SSA uses to determine if a beneficiary is making progress toward self-supporting employment.

Trial Work Period (SSDI): The trial work period is an incentive for the personal rehabilitation efforts of SSDI beneficiaries who work. The trial work period lets you test your ability to work or run a business for at least 9 months and receive full SSDI benefits (no matter how high your earnings are) if you report your work activity and your impairment does not improve.

Unincurred Business Expenses (SSDI): Support contributed to your self-employment effort by someone else. If you are self-employed, we deduct unincurred business expenses from earnings when we make a SGA decision.

Using a Ticket: The term used when a beneficiary has assigned a Ticket to an employment network or State vocational rehabilitation agency and is making timely progress toward self-supporting employment.

Unsuccessful Work Attempt (UWA) (SSDI): An effort to do substantial work (in employment or self-employment) that you stopped or reduced to below the SGA level after a short time (6 months or less). This change must have resulted because of your impairment, or the removal of special conditions related to your impairment that was essential to the further performance of your work. We do not count earnings during an unsuccessful work attempt when we make an SGA decision.

Vocational Rehabilitation Services: Those services identified in the Rehabilitation Act of 1973, as amended, that are provided by a State Vocational Rehabilitation agency (VR) in an individualized plan for employment necessary to assist an individual with a disability in preparing for, securing, retaining, or regaining an employment outcome that is consistent with the strengths, resources, priorities, concerns, abilities, capabilities, interests, and informed choice of the individual.

Workforce Investment Act of 1998 (WIA): Public Law 105-220 provides the framework for a national workforce preparation and employment system designed to meet both the needs of businesses and job seekers and those who want to further their careers. A key component of the Act enables customers to easily access the information and services they need through the One-Stop Career Center system.

Work Incentive Liaisons (WIL): Each local Social Security Administration (SSA) office has a Work Incentive Liaison (WIL) who provides advice and information about SSA's work incentive provisions and employment support programs to individuals with disabilities and outside organizations that serve those with disabilities. Contact your local SSA office for the name and telephone number of this Work Incentive Liaison.

Work Incentives: Also known as employment supports. Congress developed employment support to give individuals with disabilities assistance to move from benefit dependence to independence.

Work Incentive Planning and Assistance Program (WIPA) Project: The Social Security Administration awards grants to community-based organizations as established by Section 121 of the Ticket to Work and Work Incentives Improvement Act of 1999, Public Law 106-170. The purpose of the WIPA project is to disseminate accurate information to SSA beneficiaries with disabilities about work incentives and employment support programs to better enable them to make informed choices about work. Each WIPA project employs Community Work Incentive Coordinators.

MEDICAL CONDITIONS

Adenomyosis - a disease characterized by tumor-like masses of endometrial tissue within the muscular wall of the uterus. Has no association with endometriosis. The treatment of choice is a hysterectomy, and it is not usually disabling. This is a benign disease with no significant sequelae. A hysterectomy or medical management until after menopause resolves the symptoms.

Airway Disease (Chronic Obstructive) - increased resistance of airflow during forced expirations. This condition may be the result of narrowing or blocking of the airways due to bronchial disease or from pulmonary emphysema. This damage is usually irreversible. There may be cause for disability if there is documentation of pulmonary insufficiency with spirometric evidence. This is demonstrated by maximum voluntary ventilation (MYY) and forced expiratory volume (FEY), both equal to, or less than, the values specified corresponding to the person's height.

Amyotropic Lateral Sclerosis - a motor nerve disease in which there is muscular weakness and atrophy beginning in the hands and spreading to the forearms and legs; sensory disorders are present, and death usually occurs in 2-5 years. There is no known cure. It may be cause for disability if there are significant bulbar (pertaining to medulla oblongata) signs or significant and persistent disorganization of motor function in two extremities, resulting in sustained disturbance of gross and dexterous movements, or gait or station. There may be paresis or paralysis, tremor or other involuntary movements, ataxia (uncoordinated movement) and sensory disturbances. The assessment of impairment depends on the degree of interference with locomotion and/or interference with the use of fingers, hands and arms.

Anal Fissure - a painful sore located at the anal opening. It is more common in and usually a problem of young and middle-age adult females. The prognosis is good for most patients, but it depends upon the cause. There may be cause for disability if unresectable cancer is involved.

Anal Incontinence - the loss of voluntary control of the anal sphincter muscles. Prognosis depends on the nature of the underlying disease. In cases where involvement is strictly local and not a progressive disease, prognosis following sphincteroplasty or abdominal colostomy is quite good. A colostomy in itself is not sufficient cause for disability.

Anemia - not enough red blood cells or hemoglobin or both. Three general types are recognized: (1) iron-deficiency anemia (2) anemia due to a disturbance in the production of red blood cells in bone marrow (3) anemia due to massive blood loss due to hemorrhage or some disorder which destroys red blood cells. Prognosis is dependent upon the cause, proper treatment and how well the patient or type disorder responds to treatment. Chronic anemia (hematocrit persisting at 30% or less due to any cause) requiring one or more blood transfusions on an average of at least one every 2 months is cause for disability.

Aneurysm - the dilation or "ballooning out" of a blood vessel or a part of the heart due to the pressure of blood on weakened tissues, forming a sac of clotted blood. Any aneurysm carries the potential of rupturing and causing death or a clot dislodging and causing obstruction, irreversible damage or death. Each type of aneurysm must be treated with respect to its location, size and the general condition of the patient. Therefore, prognosis is guarded in all cases. There is cause for disability if x-rays show that there is acute or chronic dissection not controlled by prescribed medical or surgical treatment; or congestive heart failure (as described under criteria for CHF); or renal failure (as described under criteria for renal failure); or repeated syncopal episodes.

Angiosarcoma - a cancerous growth containing several dilated blood vessels. Prognosis is poor because this type tends to metastasize rapidly. There may be cause for disability with proper documentation for angiosarcoma if there is metastasis to regional lymph nodes or beyond; or if there is mycosis fungoides with lymph node or visceral involvement.

Ankylosing Spondylitis - an inflammation of the cartilage of the vertebrae and the adjacent soft tissue that is a chronic and progressive state in which the intervertebral joints become immobilized. It is often found in association with Reiter's syndrome (urethritis), arthritis, conjunctivitis, and chronic inflammatory diseases such as Crohn's disease or ulcerative colitis: Ankylosing spondylitis is a progressive form of arthritis. There may be cause for disability when there is fixation of the cervical or dorsolumbar spine at 30oor more of flexion measured from the neutral position, with x-ray evidence of calcification of the anterior and lateral ligaments; or bilateral ankylosis of the sacroiliac joints with abnormal apophyseal articulations, or generalized osteoporosis (established by x-ray) manifested by pain and limitation of back motion and paravertebral muscle spasm with x-ray evidence of either a compression fracture of a vertebral body with loss of 50% of the estimated height of the vertebral body prior to the episode or multiple fractures of vertebrae with no intervening episodes; or other vertebrogenic disorders such as herniated nucleus pulposus or spinal stenosis with pain, muscle spasm and significant limitation of motion in the spine; and appropriate radicular distribution of significant motor loss with muscular weakness and sensory and reflex loss which persisted for 3 months with prescribed therapy and expected to last at least 12 months.

Antisocial Behavior - behavior characterized by not wanting to be a part of a crowd or even a small group. The prognosis depends upon how well the patient responds to psychotherapy. There may be cause for disability if there is persistent and marked restriction of daily activities and constriction of interests and seriously impaired ability to relate to other people.

Anxiety - a functional mental disturbance caused by fear. Along with anxiety, there are physical manifestations of tachycardia, sweating and hyperventilation. These patients may go on to develop more serious psychopathology, but most respond well to counseling, psychotherapy and/or drug therapy. These patients demonstrate mental abnormalities without structural changes in brain tissue. Anxiety occurs in connection with some stressful situation.

Aortic Stenosis - constriction or narrowing of the aorta (the main, large artery leaving the heart to supply the body with oxygenated blood) that may be congenital, caused by rheumatic fever, or due to arteriosclerosis. Aortic stenosis is not clinically significant until the opening has been reduced by 35% of its original size. As the disease progresses, angina pectoris may develop, syncope upon exertion, shortness of breath, congestive heart failure and dizziness occur. Surgery is the treatment of choice. Prognosis is good if the general condition of the patient is good. Since angina pectoris (chest pain of cardiac origin) and CHF are complications of aortic stenosis, disability is assessed under those classifications.

Aphakia - an eye from which the lens has been removed; (a) monocular--0ne eye, (b) binocular-both eyes. Aphakia represents a visual handicap in addition to the loss of central visual acuity and may be a cause for disability. See Central Visual Acuity.

Aphasia - the inability to express thoughts properly via speech; (a) sensory-cannot understand spoken word, (b) motor-the muscles coordinating speech cease to function. There is cause for disability when there is organic loss of speech due to any cause, with inability to produce by any means speech which can be heard, understood and maintained.

Arrhythmia - irregular heart action causing an abnormal rhythm. The heart normally beats about 60-100 times per minute, therefore, a significant deviation results in arrhythmia. Some types of arrhythmia are: (a) atrial fibrillation, (b) atrial flutter or tachycardia, (c) ventricular fibrillation, (d) ventricular tachycardia. Recurrent episodes of arrhythmia (not due to digitalis toxicity) resulting in uncontrolled repeated episodes of cardiac syncope and documented by resting or ambulatory (Holter) EKG are grounds for disability.

Arteriosclerosis Obliterans (also called Chronic Occlusive Arterial Disease) - blockage of the arteries that supply the legs and feet. Disability exists when there is intermittent claudication with failure to visualize (on arteriogram obtained independent of Social Security disability evaluation) the common femoral or deep femoral artery in one extremity; or intermittent claudication and absence of peripheral arterial pulsations in the femoral, popliteal, dorsalis pedis, and posterior tibial arteries by doppler or plethysmography, in one extremity; or amputation at or above the tarsal region due to peripheral vascular disease.

Arthritis - a chronic syndrome characterized by inflammation of the joints (usually symmetrical) resulting in progressive destruction of joint structures. There may be generalized manifestations. Criteria for disability is: 1. Active rheumatoid arthritis and other inflammatory arthritis, with both A and B: A. Persistent joint pain, swelling, and tenderness involving multiple joints with signs of joint inflammation (heat, swelling, tenderness) despite therapy for at least 3 months, and activity expected to last over 12 months; and B. Corroboration of diagnosis at some point in time by either a positive test for the rheumatoid factor; or antinuclear antibodies; or elevated sedimentation rate. 2. Arthritis of a major weight-bearing joint (due to any cause) with limitation of motion and enlargement or effusion in the affected joint as well as a history of pain and stiffness. With gross anatomical deformity such as subluxation, contracture, bony or fibrous ankylosis, or instability; or ankylosis of the hip outside of the position of function (i.e., at least 20 or more than 30% flexion measured from the neutral position) and x-ray evidence of either joint space narrowing with osteophytosis or bony destruction (with erosions or cysts); or reconstructive surgery or surgical arthrodesis or a major weight bearing joint and return to full weight-bearing status did not occur, or is not expected to occur, within 12 months of onset. 3. Arthritis of one major joint in each of the upper extremities (due to any cause) with limitation of motion and enlargement of effusion in the affected joints as well as a history of joint pain and stiffness and X-ray evidence of either joint space narrowing with osteophytosis or bony destruction (with erosions or cysts). With abduction of both arms at the shoulders, including scapular motion, restricted to less than 90or gross anatomical deformity such as subluxation, contracture, bony or fibrous ankylosis, joint instability, or ulnar deviation. 4. Degenerative joint disease or osteoarthritis, the most common form of arthritis, is characterized by the loss of cartilage in the joint, bony destruction and inflammation. For disability scc Arthritis of a Major Weight-Bearing Joint and Arthritis in Each of the Upper Extremities.

Asthma - hyperirritability of the bronchi and trachea to certain things in one's environment. Mild attacks need no special treatment, apart from attempting to remove the offending allergens. Severe attacks require drug therapy and desensitization. Most cases can be adequately controlled. There is disability with chronic asthmatic bronchitis, documentation of pulmonary insufficiency; or episodes or severe attacks in spite of prescribed treatment, occurring at least once every 2 months, or on an average of at least 6 times a year and prolonged expiration with wheezing and rhonchi between attacks.

Atherosclerosis - condition in which the inner layer of an artery wall becomes thick and irregular from accumulation of fatty deposits. Coronary artery disease is the most common type of heart disease and is the leading cause of death in the United States and other countries. Atherosclerosis particularly affects the coronary, cerebral and peripheral arteries. Disability is evaluated under the system that is affected.

Atopic Dermatitis - a form of hereditary allergic inflammation of the skin that involves itching and inflammation of the skin. There may be cause for disability with extensive lesions, including involvement of the hands and the feet which impose a severe limitation of function and which are not responding to prescribed treatment.

Atrial Fibrillation - 0ccurs when the atria fail to contract effectively. This condition is frequent in chronic organic heart disease. The patient experiences palpitations and irregular heartbeats of 160-220 beats per minute. A major complication is formation of clots in the left atrium. Electrical cardioversion is the treatment of choice because control of the ventricular rate is most important. Prognosis is best in transient cases as it becomes worse with longer episodes, congestive heart failure, atrial enlargement, and the general extent of organic heart disease. See criteria for disability under Atrioventricular Dissociation.

Atrial Flutter - a condition resulting from some degree of A V block wherein the atria contract at a rate of 250-300 beats per minute, while the ventricles maintain a much slower rate. This condition most commonly accompanies rheumatic mitral stenosis, thyrotoxicosis, coronary disease and atrial septal defect. This condition is more serious than atrial fibrillation and may lead to ventricular strain, ischemia or infarction. See criteria for disability under Atrioventricular Dissociation. It also may be evaluated under ischemic heart disease or myocardial infarction if these develop as complications.

Atrioventricular Dissociation (A V Block) - occurs when the, atria and the ventricles receive signals from different pacemakers. There are first-, second-, and third-degree blocks. A. First-Degree Block-only a delay in A V conduction. It may be due to digitalis intoxication, inflammation, toxins, degenerative disease of the heart or to increased vagal tone. First- degree heart block requires no treatment except for the underlying condition. B. Second-Degree Block-occurs when there is a delay in A V conduction plus some dropped beats. There are 2 types: (1) Mobitz Type I-caused by increased vagal tone, is a frequent complication of myocardial infarction; requires no treatment unless there is a blood-flow disturbance. (2) Mobitz Type II-usually caused by a conduction block or myocardial infarction or myocarditis. There is extreme syncope due to abrupt temporary cessation or diminution of blood flow. This can be fatal. C. Third-Degree Block-a complete A V block which may follow second-degree block, accidental surgical trauma, myocardial infarction or it may be congenital. Prognosis is uncertain. Without a pacemaker, the patient (Mobitz Type II and complete A V Block) lives less than a year. In left coronary insufficiency, mortality is very high even with a pacemaker and proper therapy. Recurrent arrhythmias may be cause for disability if they are not due to digitalis toxicity and result in uncontrolled, repeated episodes of cardiac syncope and are documented by resting or ambulatory EKG readings.

Back Pain - pain that may be due to simple muscle strain or spasm, but there are many other causes. It is often a symptom of other diseases such as renal disease, prostate in men, pelvic organ disorders in women, or disease or disorder in other abdominal structures. If there is a disability, it is based upon the underlying cause of the pain.

Bladder Cancer - usually occurs between ages 55-65 and is more prevalent in male cigarette smokers. There is a 5-year survival rate in about 80% of the patients where there is no invasion of bladder muscle, but it drops to 10% where there is invasion. There is disability in cases of urinary bladder carcinoma with infiltration beyond the bladder wall; or metastasis; or if unresectable; or with recurrence after total cystectomy.

Brain Tumors - malignant tumors of the brain. All malignant gliomas, (astrocytoma-grades III and IV, glioblastoma multiforme), medulloblastoma, ependymoblastoma, or primary sarcoma; or astrocytoma (grades land 11), meningioma, pituitary tumors, oligodendrogliomas, ependymoma, clivus chordoma are reasons for disability. Characteristic symptoms are headache, vomiting, personality changes, papilledema, convulsive seizures, drowsiness, lethargy and changes in temperature, pulse or respirations. Surgery is the best treatment, but many are inoperable by the time they are diagnosed. Primary intracranial neoplasms (brain tumors) are divided into 6 classes: 1. Tumors of the skull: osteoma, hemangioma, granuloma, xanthoma, osteitis deformans. 2. Tumors of the meninges (the 3 membranes covering the brain and spinal cord): meningioma, sarcoma, gliomatosis. 3. Tumors of the cranial nerves: glioma of the optic nerve, schwannoma (neurilemoma) of the 8th and 5th cranial nerves. 4. Tumors of the supportive tissue: gliomas. 5. Tumors of the pituitary and pineal bodies: pituitary adenoma, pinealoma. 6. Congenital tumors: craniopharyngioma, chordoma, germinoma, teratoma, dermoid cyst, angioma and hemangioblastoma.

Bronchiectasis - enlargement of one or both bronchi usually accompanied by secretion of large amounts of foul smelling pus. Treatment usually consists of oxygen, postural drainage, bronchoscopic removal of secretions, and surgery for lesions not responsive to medical treatment. Bronchiectasis may be reason for disability when demonstrated by x-ray and episodes of acute bronchitis or pneumonia or hemoptysis occurring at least once every 2 months; or impairment of pulmonary function.

Bullous Pemphigoid - may be acute or chronic) a disease which affects adults characterized by the sudden appearance of large blisters on the skin (which up to this point appeared normal) and which leave pigmented spots when the blisters leave. This condition may be accompanied by itching, burning and general constitutional disturbances. The cause is not known. There may be cause for disability when the bullous pemphigoid is extensive and does not respond to prescribed treatment.

Cancer Metastatic to the Liver - usually clinically silent. The patient usually has symptoms only of the primary lesion. Any tumor except primary brain tumors can metastasize to the liver. There is no effective treatment known at present and the prognosis is dependent upon the primary cancer. There is disability in cases of primary or metastatic malignant tumors of the liver; or carcinoma of the gallbladder; or carcinoma of the bile ducts, unresectable or with metastases.

Cancer of the Fallopian Tubes - the tubes or oviducts through which eggs pass from the ovaries to the uterus, Primary cancer in the fallopian tubes is rare, usually unilateral, and difficult to diagnose preoperatively, Survival rate beyond 5 years is very poor. It is cause for disability if it is unresectable or with metastasis.

Cancer of the Pancreas - most prevalent in those over 40. Characterized by jaundice, weight loss, loss of appetite, nausea and pain (if present, is in mid-back and is relieved by standing or clasping the knees while sitting). Prognosis is very poor in all cases; few survive 5 years. There is disability for carcinoma of the pancreas except Isle of Langerhans carcinoma, unless the Isle of Langerhans carcinoma is inoperable and active.

Cancer of the Uterus - a malignancy that arises in the endometrium and is usually postmenopausal. It constitutes disability if it is inoperable and not controlled by prescribed therapy; or recurrent after total hysterectomy; or with total pelvic exenteration.

Carcinoma of the Colon and Rectum - one of the leading causes of cancer death. Older persons are most affected-especially those in their 70's. It is usually a malignant transformation of either ulcerative colitis or certain types of colonic polyps. When there is no metastasis, more than 70% survive 5 years. Patients with an overall rectal involvement have a lower survival rate. The majority of all the surgical patients will eventually have recurrent disease and most will die of it. Chemotherapy and radiation are not very successful in recurrent cases. There is a disability when it is inoperable, or there is metastasis or it recurs.

Carcinoma of the Kidney (also called Hypernephroma) - the most common type of cancer of the kidney in adults. A nephrectomy and removal of metastasis when possible is the treatment of choice. There is a 10-year survival in about 10%, much less in others. There may be disability when it is unresectable; or with metastasis.

Carcinoma of the Stomach - cancer of the stomach believed to be caused from something in the environment. Genetics may be a slight factor. Surgical resection, when possible, is the definitive treatment. The prognosis depends upon the extent of this malignancy and metastasis. Disability only if inoperable.

Carotid Artery Arteriosclerosis - the narrowing of the carotid arteries due to fatty deposits in the walls of the arteries. There may be paralysis on the side of the body supplied, speech impairment, or blindness. Usually there is some permanent damage. If the patient is treated surgically, the prognosis is excellent. Medical management is less effective. Disability is dependent upon the degree of permanent damage. It is evaluated under the body system affected.

Cataract - a progressive hardening and clouding of the lens with or without the inclusion of the capsule. A.

Lenticular cataract-affects the lens. B. Capsular cataract-affects the capsule. C. Capsolenticular cataract-affects both lens and capsule. A cataract may be (1) hard, soft or fluid (2) partial or complete or (3) stationary or progressive. If surgery is successful, vision is restored with contacts or glasses. Disability depends upon the degree of impairment.

Central Visual Acuity (Loss of) - pertains to how clearly one sees from the fovea centralis (center of retina). It may be caused by impaired distant and/ or near vision. Disability exists when remaining vision in the better eye after best correction is 20/200 or less.

Cerebral Palsy - temporary or permanent loss of the ability to move or to control movement or the loss of sensation. There is disability with an IQ of 69 or less; or abnormal behavior patterns, such as destructiveness or emotional instability; or significant interference in communication due to speech, hearing, or visual defect; or disorganization of motor function.

Cerebrovascular Accident (Stroke, CVA) - involves the cessation of blood flow to apart of the brain with subsequent local destruction of brain tissue, in most cases. The sudden and dramatic neurological deficit appears within seconds, minutes or occasionally hours. CV A may involve thrombosis, embolism, thromboembolism, hypertensive hemorrhage, ruptured aneurysm, etc. The symptoms and physical findings reflect the location of the lesion I. Strokes due to occlusion of: A. Internal carotid artery-may be asymptomatic or so severe as to cause death in a few days. Frequently blindness in one eye and then the other is a warning sign. Other symptoms are opposite-side paralysis and speech disorders. B. Middle cerebral artery-opposite-side paralysis, numbness in limbs, blindness in one eye, inability to understand spoken words or the inability to speak. C. Anterior cerebral artery-sensorimotor deficit in the opposite foot, leg or arm, and changes in the usual behavior pattern. D. Posterior cerebral artery-may produce uncontrollable jerking or shaking movement, eyes paralyzed in a stare, coma and monocular blindness. II. Other causes of cerebrovascular accident (CV A): A. Stroke due to embolism-less common; usually develops rapidly within one minute. Headache, blindness and paralysis develop instantly. B. Intracranial hemorrhage-begins with a headache, then over a period of several hours there is slurred speech, paralysis of limbs and face, vomiting, vertigo, loss of control of gaze and then coma. The threat of a recurrence is very high except in the case of intracranial hemorrhage. Most neurological deficits are not greatly helped by physical therapy except for speech disorders. Massive strokes usually result in death in a matter of hours.

Cervical Cancer - a noninvasive cancer of the cervix (the neck of the uterus). One of the most common malignancies of the female reproductive system. For this reason, regular Pap smears are important for early diagnosis and treatment. There are 5 classes recognized: Class I-no abnormal or atypical cells Class II-benign atypical cells present Class III-atypical cells with suspicion of malignancy Class IV - malignant cells present Class V -large numbers of malignant cells. Classes I and II need no treatment other than regular Pap smears. Classes III, IV and V should be followed by a biopsy of the cervix to determine if there is evidence of invasive disease. If so, more evaluation is needed of the lungs, gastrointestinal tract, urinary tract and lymph nodes. For carcinoma in situ (cancer that is localized), nearly 100% are completely cured. For more invasive lesions, less than 10% survive 5 years after diagnosis. It is in this latter 10% that there may be cause for disability because it eventually becomes uncontrollable by prescribed therapy.

Cervical Radiculopathies - pain caused by pinched nerves in the cervical spine (neck). The pain radiates from the neck to the hand arid may be accompanied by weakness. Cases with no complications usually show improvement in two weeks with proper bed rest, analgesics and anti-inflammatory drugs. Prognosis is also good where a laminectomy (repair of herniated disc) is required. When atrophy of muscles has occurred, prognosis is not so good. Disability exists when there is significant loss of use (motor loss) of the hand along with muscular weakness, sensory and reflex loss.

Cervical Spinal Injury - an injury to the spinal cord in the neck, usually the result of an automobile accident, sports-related accident or assault. There is usually loss of sensation below the injury and paralysis. The prognosis depends upon the extent and location of the injury. When the spinal cord is completely severed, prognosis is poor for restoration of function. An injury at or above cervical vertebra C3 is usually associated with paralysis of the diaphragm and a respirator is necessary to keep the patient alive. Disability is evaluated according to the degree of impairment.

Chest Pain of Cardiac Origin - pain which is precipitated by effort and promptly relieved by sublingual nitroglycerine or rapid acting nitrates or rest. The character of the pain is described as crushing, squeezing, burning or oppressive pain in the chest. In order for chest pain of cardiac origin to qualify as a disability there must be substantiated evidence: treadmill exercise test, horizontal or down-sloping ischemic depression of the ST segment to 1.0 mm or greater; or, multiform, bidirectional or sequentially described premature ventricular systoles; or transmural myocardial infarction (ERG); or resting ERG showing ischemic disease; or development of second- or third-degree heart block; or angiographic evidence of narrowing of the coronary arteries.

Chronic Brain Syndrome (Organic Brain Syndrome) - results from chronic irreversible impairment of cerebral tissue function. Impairment is usually permanent and may be progressive. The degree of impairment may range from mild to severe. Acute brain syndromes are temporary and reversible conditions with favorable prognosis and no significant residual effects. Occasionally, an acute brain syndrome may progress to chronic. There is cause for disability when there is demonstrated deterioration in intellectual functioning, manifested by persistence in one or more of the following: marked memory defect for recent events; or impoverished, slowed or perseverative thinking with confusion or disorientation; or labile, shallow, or coarse affect; and resulting persistence of marked restriction of daily activities and constriction of interests and deterioration in personal habits and seriously impaired ability to relate to other people.

Chronic Bronchitis - a chronic productive cough for at least 3 months during 2 consecutive years. The most important cause is smoking. No smoking, antibiotics, postural drainage and plenty of fluids are the usual course of treatment. Prognosis depends upon the degree of impaired respiratory function. When there is severe impairment with carbon dioxide retention, most live less than 5 years. Episodes of severe attacks in spite of prescribed treatment, occurring at least once every 2 months, or on an average of at least 6 times a year and prolonged expiration with wheezing or rhonchi (a rattling sound) between attacks is reason for disability.

Chronic Venous Insufficiency - (of the lower extremities) occurs after thrombophlebitis in the deep leg veins and is characterized by edema and dilated superficial veins. The patient must wear elastic hose to control the edema. Complications which may arise are pigmentation around the ankle, varicose veins, dermatitis and ulceration. There may be disability for chronic venous insufficiency of the lower extremities with incompetency or obstruction of the deep venous return, associated with varicose veins, extensive edema, dermatitis, and recurrent or persistent ulceration which has not healed following 3 months of prescribed medical or surgical treatment.

Cirrhosis - diffuse liver disease in which there is fibrosis, formation of nodules and loss of liver function. Cirrhosis leads to: portal hypertension, fluid retention, kidney failure and hepatic coma. A. Biliary Cirrhosis-cirrhosis due to destruction or obstruction of the bile ducts. Surgical relief of the obstruction in secondary biliary cirrhosis is the treatment of choice. There is no known cure for primary biliary cirrhosis; one can only relieve the symptoms by a high calorie, balanced diet and give vitamins A, D, and K, etc. 1. Secondary-caused by some kind of obstruction in the bile ducts which can be treated surgically or medically. 2. Primary-marked by a gradual deterioration, ascites and massive upper GI hemorrhage which is terminal. There is no known cure, it is slowly progressive, and only the symptoms can be relieved. B. Laennec's Cirrhosis-a diffuse finely scarring form most often associated with alcoholism and a poor diet. There is no cure, but the process can be slowed by denial of alcohol and a balanced diet. If the patient abstains from alcohol his 5-year survival rate is 60%; if not, 40%. Massive hemorrhage from esophageal varices is the major cause of death. Chronic liver disease (portal, post necrotic, biliary cirrhosis, Laennec's cirrhosis, chronic active hepatitis) qualifies as a dis- ability with x-ray or endoscopic evidence of esophageal varices and accompanying massive hemorrhages due to these varices; or serum bilirubin of 2.5 mg per 100 cc or greater for at least 5 months; or performance of a shunt operation for the esophageal varices; or liver dysfunction; or confirmation by a liver biopsy; or ascites not attributable to other causes which is recurring or persistent for at least 3 months and demonstrated by abdominal paracentesis; or persistent hypoalbuminuria of 3.0 gm per 100 cc or less; or hepatic cell necrosis or inflammation persisting for 3 months documented by repeated abnormalities of prothrombin time and enzymes indicative of liver dysfunction.

Coagulation Defects - any breakdown in the blood clotting process that results in an abnormal tendency to bleed. For normal clotting to occur, there is combined activity of vascular, platelet and plasma factors. The vascular factor refers to the natural immediate reaction of blood vessels to constrict where injured. The platelets are a component of blood that begin to adhere to and plug injured sites and that release certain substances that finish the coagulation process. These are the coagulation factors which are plasma proteins (fibrinogen and prothrombin) as well as thromboplastin and calcium. This condition does not constitute a disability unless it is extreme, such as hemophilia. Many liver disorders cause coagulation defects. For those patients with heart or vascular diseases and who must take anticoagulant drugs, this is a problem. The treatment and prognosis depend upon the underlying cause. Even therapy with antihemophilic globulin (AHG) does not constitute a disability. Coagulation defects with spontaneous hemorrhage requiring transfusion at least 3 times during the 5 months prior to adjudication is cause for disability.

Congestive Heart Failure (CHF) - cessation of the heart's action due to the presence of congestion (usually fluid in the lungs and/or around the heart in the pericardium) or vascular congestion. Heart failure may be left or right sided, may develop gradually or may be sudden with acute pulmonary edema. Left ventricular failure manifests as tachycardia, fatigue with exertion, intolerance to cold, recurring nocturnal short- ness of breath, cough, rusty tinged or brownish sputum, palpable and audible 3rd and 4th heart sounds, rales and pleural effusion. Acute pulmonary edema occurs suddenly and is life threatening. There is extreme cyanosis, shallow, irregular breathing, restlessness, thready pulse, blood pressure difficult to find, wheezing and rales. Treatment must be immediate or death is certain. Symptoms of right ventricular failure are tired feeling, feeling of fullness in the neck, fullness in the abdomen, sometimes pain in the upper abdomen, swelling around the ankles, hepatomegaly, and cyanosis in the nails. There are no specific findings on EKG for CHF, but chest x-rays are helpful in evaluating its presence and possible cause. Disability exists if CHF is manifested by evidence of vascular congestion such as hepatomegaly, peripheral or pulmonary edema with: persistent CHF on clinical examination despite prescribed therapy; or persistent left ventricular enlargement and hypertrophy documented by both extension of the cardiac shadow (left ventricle) to the vertebral column on a left lateral chest x-ray or PA chest x-ray or certain E KG findings; or persistent "mitral heart involvement" documented by double shadow on PA chest x-ray (or characteristic distortion of barium-filled esophagus) and either: 1. EKG showing QRS duration less than 0.12 second with SVl plus Rv5 (or Rv6) of 35 mm or greater and ST segment depressed more than 0.5 mm and low diphasic or inverted T waves in leads with tall R waves; or 2. E KG evidence of right ventricular hypertrophy with R wave of 5.0 mm or greater in lead V 1 and progressive decrease in R/S amplitude from lead V 2 to V 6 or V 6; or Cor pulmonale (chronic) documented by both: 1. Right ventricular enlargement (or prominence of the right out-flow tract) or chest x-ray or fluoroscopy; and 2. EKG evidence of right ventricular hypertrophy with R wave of 5.0 mm or greater in lead V 1 to V 6 or V 6.

Convulsive Disorders - any disease or disorder which may produce convulsions. Some are: epilepsy, eclampsia, tetanus, meningitis, uremia, poisoning of dietary origin, syphilis, heat stroke, metabolic disturbances, etc. The seizures for most of these conditions are temporary and end when the illness ends. The exceptions are epilepsy and in cases where a permanent lesion is left in the brain. In such cases, the seizures are recurring, but usually controllable by proper medication. There is no disability unless the convulsive disorder is classified as epilepsy and meets the SSA requirements.

Cor Pulmonale (CP) - the enlargement of the right ventricle due to lung disease or disorder. Acute cor pulmonale results from pulmonary embolism. Chronic cor pulmonale is the result of prolonged pulmonary dysfunction or disease (chronic bronchitis, emphysema, surgery, or trauma, etc.). Some symptoms and signs of chronic CP are shortness of breath, syncope on exertion, x-ray showing ventricular enlargement and enlargement of pulmonary arteries, E KG evidence, gallop rhythm, distended jugular veins (in - neck), hepatomegaly, edema, cough, cyanosis, wheezing and substernal pain. Acute CP shows the symptoms of a pulmonary embolism in which a clot becomes lodged in the pulmonary artery blocking the flow of blood from the heart to the lungs. The embolus is usually from a thromboembolus formed in a deep leg vein, but may be from a congenital heart disease, some systemic disease, oral contraceptives, injury or surgery. Some symptoms are: shortness of breath, breathlessness, rapid and shallow respirations, anxiety, restlessness, apprehension, pulmonary hypertension, dull substernal pain, light-headedness, syncope, convulsions, neurological impairments, cyanosis, cough, hemoptysis, pleuritic chest pain, fever, and/ or pleural effusion. Chronic CP may be cause for disability when there is documented pulmonary insufficiency or accompanying CHF (chronic).

Crohn's Disease - Regional Enteritis (another name for Crohn's Disease).

Cystic Fibrosis - a congenital condition where there is gradual fibrosis of the pancreas, changes in the respiratory tree which causes obstructions in the lungs and abnormal sweat chloride levels, fatty stools and rectal prolapse. It is usually fatal in early childhood, but a few do make it to adulthood. Disability is based upon the degree of impairment of the particular body system that is affected the most.

Deaf Mutism - the condition that exists when one cannot hear or speak. Cases of alleged "deaf mutism" should be documented by a hearing evaluation. If they qualify, then disability is in order.

Deep Mycotic Infection - a deep infection caused by a microorganism affecting the deep layers of the skin. There may be disability when there is extensive spreading and the lesions do not respond to prescribed treatment.

Delusions - a belief in something that is not real; such as when one imagines he is Adolf Hitler. There is cause for disability when there is resulting persistence of marked restriction of daily activities and constriction of interests and seriously impaired ability to relate to others. It is considered Functional Psychotic Disorders for a disability.

Depression - a mental disorder wherein one is very sad, seems to have lost hope, and lacks feelings of self-worth. A. Reactive depression-a state of depression in reaction to some personal loss such as the death of a loved one. It is characterized by symptoms of hopelessness, lack of interest in one's own life, inability to manage daily affairs, a sense of guilt and behavior in a manner unlike the usual self. Certain diseases predispose to reactive depression: myocardial infarction, Parkinson's disease, cancer and multiple sclerosis. B. Manic depression-usually affects those in middle and late adulthood. The patient alternates between periods of deep depression and great excitement. These patients are often suicidal when in the depression stage. C. Involutional melancholia-this disorder most often affects elderly females of low socioeconomic background. As their intellectual and physical abilities begin to decrease, these patients are unable to stay in touch with reality. The main danger in all forms of depression is suicide. The majority of all these can be successfully treated by psychoanalysis, electroconvulsive therapy (ECT) and/ or drugs. There may be a disability if the patient does not respond to treatment.

Dermatitis Herpetiformis - a chronic eruption of inflamed, blister-like, intensely itching and burning pimples that appear on the elbows, knees, sacrum, buttocks, back of the neck, face and head. This is fairly uncommon and usually affects 15-60-year-olds. Disability exists when the lesions are extensive and do not respond to prescribed treatment.

Detached Retina - the retina becomes separated from the underlying layer and there is complete loss of vision where the retina is detached. If surgical repair of the retina is successful, good results are obtained. There may be a recurrence. Disability is based upon loss of visual efficiency. Visual efficiency of the better eye after best correction is 20% or less. (The percent of remaining visual efficiency equals the product of the percent of remaining central visual efficiency and the percent of remaining visual field efficiency).

Diabetes Insipidus (or Polyuria) - the patient produces large quantities of urine that is pale and watery, usually occurs in the young and is secondary to tumors of the pituitary or head injury, etc. Dehydration is a constant danger. A. Nephrogenic diabetes insipidus-an inherited condition in which kidney function is normal except for the ability to concentrate urine. B. Vasopressin-sensitive diabetes insipidus-a chronic or temporary disorder caused by a deficiency of vasopressin (ADH) and characterized by the production of excessive amounts of dilute urine and extreme thirst. This is caused by injury or tumors of the pituitary gland. There may be cause for disability with a urine specific gravity of 1.005 or below, persistent for at least 3 months with recurrent dehydration.

Diabetes Mellitus - a metabolic disease caused by an insufficient insulin secretion from the Isle of Langerhans of the pancreas which results in an elevated blood sugar. There are two forms: A. Juvenile-the onset is during childhood or early teens. There is frequent urination, extreme thirst, hunger, fatigue, weakness and weight loss. It requires intramuscular (IM) injections of insulin and it is difficult to control. B. Mature-the onset is during adulthood; fatigue, weight loss, blurred vision, impotency, nonhealing sores and the feet may be insensitive to pain. This form is more easily controlled by diet and oral or injected insulin. The longer a patient has diabetes, the more likely he is to experience complications. The most common chronic ones are: diabetic retinopathy, kidney disorders and nerve disorders. Acute complications are ketoacidosis and coma. There is cause for disability with neuropathy demonstrated by significant and persistent disorganization of motor function in two extremities resulting in sustained disturbance of gross dexterous movements, or gait and station; or acidosis occurring at least on the average of once every 2 months documented by appropriate blood chemical tests (pH, pCO3 or bicarbonate levels); or amputation at, or above, the tarsal (toe) region due to diabetic necrosis or peripheral vascular disease; or retinitis proliferans.

Disseminated Lupus Erythematosus - that affects the whole system in which there is inflammation of the skin with scaly patches. Respiratory infections, pleurisy, pleural effusion, pericarditis, arthritis, endocarditis and nephrotic syndrome accompany DLE. DLE may be reason for disability when it is established by a positive LE preparation or biopsy or positive antinuclear antibody (ANA) test, and there is involvement of renal or cardiac or pulmonary or gastrointestinal or central nervous system on a frequent basis.

Down's Syndrome (Mongolism) - a genetic disorder wherein the child is born with a small head and a broad face, an abnormally large distance between the eyes, flattening of parts of the skull, a protuberant tongue, low set ears and varying degrees of mental retardation. The prognosis depends upon the degree of mental impairment, but usually I can expect a near normal life span. Disability depends upon IQ and marked dependence on others for personal needs.
Dumping Syndrome - ingested food is dumped into the jejunum too quickly after eating. This happens after gastric surgery in some cases. It may cause symptoms of weakness, dizziness, sweating, nausea, vomiting and palpitations soon after eating. Within about two hours diarrhea sets in. This condition usually responds to treatment and is generally not cause for disability unless it is recurrent and/ or persistent despite treatment.

Duodenal Ulcer - a local destruction of mucosa in the duodenum by peptic secretions. About 4/5 are managed successfully medically. In the other 1/5, surgery is eventually needed. Possible complications of surgery are calcium deficiency, anemia, bowel obstruction, continuing pain and the dumping syndrome. Disability exists when peptic ulcer disease is demonstrated by x-ray or endoscopy with recurrent ulceration after definitive surgery or is persistent despite therapy; or inoperable fistula formation; or recurrent obstruction demonstrated by x-ray or endoscopy; or weight loss due to this disease.

Dysidrosis - a disorder of the sweat glands which never affects children or the aged. The contents of the sweat glands are retained. Presence of the disorder with extensive lesions which are not responding to prescribed treatment, including involvement of the hands or feet which imposes a severe limitation of function constitutes a disability.

Edema - swelling due to an excess accumulation of fluid. A. Renal-edema caused by kidney disorder or disease. B. Pretibial-edema over the tibia of the lower leg. C. Preorbital-edema around the eye. D. Pulmonary-swelling or retention of fluid in the lungs due to disease or injury. Edema in itself is not a disease but rather a symptom of some other disease or disorder. Therefore, disability is based upon the underlying condition or disease.

Emphysema - distention of the air spaces in the lungs. It is usually caused by smoking and there is a genetic predisposition in those patients with a deficiency of the enzyme Alpha-l-Antitrypsin. Treatment consists of not smoking and an attempt to stop its progression. Early treatment of respiratory ailments is a must. Prognosis is dependent upon the degree of parenchymal destruction as this is irreversible. There is a gradual progression of shortness of breath. (Parenchyma-refers to the essential parts of an organ.) Disability depends upon the degree of pulmonary insufficiency and accompanying (usually) cor pulmonale properly documented.

End Organ Damage - damage to the heart, brain, kidneys or retinae due to injury or disease. If a disability exists, it depends upon the disease or disorder, the organ involved, and the degree of impairment.

Endometrial Cancer - an invasive malignancy of the inner lining of the uterus. It is usually postmenopausal and is best diagnosed by biopsy. The treatment of choice is a total hysterectomy with the majority of the patients being completely cured.

Enteritis (Regional) - inflammation of the small intestine. For disability, regional enteritis must be demonstrated by barium studies, biopsy, or endoscopy and with: persistent or recurrent intestinal obstruction evidenced by abdominal pain, distention, nausea, and vomiting and accompanied by stenotic areas of small bowel with proximal intestinal dilation; or persistent or recurrent systemic manifestations such as arthritis, iritis, fever, or liver dysfunction, not attributable to other causes; or intermittent obstruction due to intractable abscess or fistula formation; or significant weight loss. Other names for regional enteritis are: granulomatous ileitis, ileocolitis, and Crohn's disease.

Epidermoid Carcinoma of the Anus - cancer of the anus. This type of carcinoma usually develops silently and by the time it is diagnosed, it has metastasized to the regional lymph nodes and beyond. Disability exists when the cancer is inoperable; or there is metastasis beyond the regional lymph nodes; or recurrence and metastasis after resection.

Epilepsy - a disturbance of the consciousness during which generalized convulsions may occur. It is episodal in nature. There are four main types: A. Grand mal-often preceded by an aura followed by convulsions, unconsciousness, frothing at the mouth and the face turns blue. B. Petit mal-very mild in nature and lasts only a short time. Those around may be unaware of any change in the person. C. Psychomotor-an aura is experienced immediately before the seizure, the patient is unable to respond to simple questions, may continue a previously commenced action, there is convulsive movement of the lips, head, or arms, may become violent if restrained and the attacks last for varying lengths of time. D. Focal motor seizures-the patient usually remains conscious unless motor activity becomes generalized. The convulsive movement is usually limited to just one limb or one side of the body. Most epileptics show no evidence of mental deterioration and with appropriate therapy experience a decrease in frequency or a complete cessation of seizures. In cases of secondary epilepsy, the prognosis depends upon the underlying disease. Disability for grand mal seizures or psychomotor: documentation by EEG and by detailed description of a typical seizure pattern, including all associated phenomena; occurring more frequently than once a month, in spite of at least 3 months of prescribed treatment, with: diurnal episodes (loss of consciousness and convulsive seizures); or nocturnal episodes manifesting residuals which interfere significantly with activities during the day. Disability for minor motor seizures (petit mal, psychomotor, or focal): documentation by EEG and by detailed description of a typical seizure pattern, including all associated phenomena; occurring more frequently than once weekly in spite of at least 3 months prescribed treatment.

Erythema - red spots covering the skin caused by capillary congestion. There are many different kinds and they arise from a variety of causes. It is disabling when the lesions are extensive and do not respond to prescribed treatment.

Exfoliative Dermatitis - (acute or subacute) a very severe, generalized skin disorder with red spots and scaling. This is a potentially life-threatening disease and recurrences are frequent. The exact cause is unknown and onset is rapid. There is a disability with extensive lesions not responding to prescribed treatment.

Fibrosis - abnormal formation of fiber-like tissue or scar tissue. A. Pulmonary fibrosis-scar tissue that forms in the lungs after inflammation, pneumonia and TB. B. Focal fibrosis-fibrosis in isolated spots or areas. C. Disseminated fibrosis-fibrosis that is generalized or widespread throughout most of the lung or other organ. D. Interstitial fibrosis-fibrosis in the air sacs (alveoli) of the lungs. Fibrosis is progressive and debilitating. There is no known cure unless the affected part can be excised and then there may be recurrence. Disability depends upon the system involved and the degree of impairment.

Field of Vision - the "field" or space within which an object can be seen without moving the head and keeping the eyes on a fixed point. Disability exists when there is contraction of the peripheral visual fields in the better eye to 10¡ or less from the point of fixation; or so the widest diameter subtends an angle no greater than 20%; or to 20% or less visual field efficiency.

Fistula in Ano - a track or passage leading from the anal canal to the skin near the anal opening. Most of the time these are secondary to anorectal abscesses or to operations or anal fissures (a tear in the lower anal canal). Fistulas may be single or multiple with a purulent drainage and recurring abscess formation. They may also indicate regional enteritis or colitis. If the fistula is secondary, the primary cause must be treated or the fistula will not heal. Primary fistula in ano is treated best by surgical excision. A permanent or temporary colostomy may be necessary. It is grounds for disability only when persistent and does not respond to treatment.

Functional Non-Psychotic Disorders - characterized by demonstrable mental abnormalities without structural changes in brain tissue. Disorders that fall into this category are psychophysiological: anxiety, depressive neurosis, paranoia, schizophrenia, hysteria, antisocial behavior, passive-aggressive behavior, inadequate personality, sexual deviation, alcohol and drug addiction. All of the above disorders may constitute disability if they are persistent. (See entry on Neurosis).

Gastrectomy - surgical removal of part or all of the stomach. A. Total gastrectomy-removal of the whole stomach. B. Partial gastrectomy-removal of a portion of the stomach. Indications for gastrectomy are perforation of an ulcer, obstruction that does not respond to medical management, hemorrhage (2 or more major ones), malignancy, etc. The type of surgery (partial or total) depends upon the patient's condition and the disease. The "dumping syndrome," anemia, weight loss and diarrhea are complications after such surgery. The condition that necessitated surgery is often recurrent. Disability exists in peptic ulcer disease (demonstrated by x-ray or endoscopy), with: recurrent ulceration after definitive surgery persistent despite therapy; or inoperable fistula formation; or recurrent obstruction demonstrated by x-ray or endoscopy; or extreme weight loss.

Gastric Ulcer - small, localized destruction of the mucosa by peptic secretion in the antrum body or prepyloric region of the stomach. If malignant, a gastric resection should be done; if benign, treat it medically. Gastric ulcers recur more often and are more likely to require surgery than duodenal ulcers. Disability requirements are the same as those outlined in the entry for gastrectomy under Peptic Ulcer Disease.

Glaucoma - pressure inside the eye. 1. Primary a. Angle-closure glaucoma- (also known as acute, uncompensated, iris block, narrow-angle and congestive glaucoma). The shallow anterior chamber is congested due to all extreme anterior attachment of the iris to the ciliary body thus blocking outflow of aqueous humor. b. Open-angle glaucoma- (also called simple, chronic, compensated, wide-angle, and glaucoma simplex). There is a disturbance in the flow of aqueous humor between the anterior chamber and the canal of Schlemm. 2. Secondary-results from a preexisting disease. Primary open-angle glaucoma should be managed medically and prognosis is good if the patient follows instructions. Surgery is the definitive treatment for angle-closure glaucoma and these patients do well. Prognosis in secondary glaucoma depends upon the extent of the underlying disease. Disability depends upon the degree of visual impairment.

Goodpasture's Syndrome - an antiglomerular basement membrane disease with lung and kidney complications. The condition is terminal and progression is rapid. This disease most often affects young males and is characterized by severe hemoptysis, shortness of breath, iron deficiency anemia, hematuria, proteinuria and rapidly progressive renal failure. There is no known cure.

Granulocytopenia (Chronic) - a chronic reduction in blood granulocytes resulting in increased susceptibility to bacterial infections and ulcers in proportion to the duration and severity of the granulocytopenia. There is a history of multiple focal skin infections, perirectal region infections and respiratory infections. Severe granulocytopenia lasting longer than four weeks usually results in death. There is cause for disability with absolute neutrophil counts repeatedly below 1,000 cells per cubic millimeter; and documented recurrent systemic bacterial infections occurring at least three times during the five months prior to adjudication.

Groin Hernias (Femoral, Inguinal) - the abnormal bulging or protruding of a structure from its normal place through a congenital or acquired place. An external truss is of no value; surgery is the definitive treatment. A. Femoral- the descending of the intestines and femoral vessels through the femoral ring (over the legs). B. Inguinal-the intestines pass through the inguinal canal (the most common). Prognosis is excellent unless it has become strangulated and gangrene has set in. There is no cause for disability.

Hansen's Disease (Leprosy) - a slowly progressive, infectious disease that causes lesions of the skin or nerve tissue. Leprosy is classified as a disability as an active disease or considered as "under a disability" while hospitalized.

Head and Neck (Malignancies) - There is cause for disability if it is inoperable; or not controlled by prescribed therapy; or recurrent after radical surgery or irradiation; or with distant metastasis; or epidermoid carcinoma occurring in the pyriform sinus or posterior third of the tongue.

Heart Block - a condition in which the electrical impulses which travel through the heart's special conduction system to trigger heartbeat is slowed or blocked to such a degree that an artificial pacemaker is required to keep the patient alive. (See Atrioventricular Dissociation for disability criteria, further definition and classification.)

Heart Failure - occurs when the heart cannot pump sufficient blood to meet the needs of the body. This is a condition secondary to a preexisting disease or dysfunction. The treatment is first aimed at the underlying cause, then reduce the cardiac workload, reduce fluid retention and increase contractility of the heart. Acute pulmonary edema should be treated as a medical emergency. Prognosis is dependent upon the underlying disease. Disability exists with diagnosis and proper documentation of the impairment. See Congestive Heart Failure.

Hemodialysis - a process of purifying the blood, outside the body, of wastes normally excreted through the kidneys. Due to some disorder this normal process. has been hampered or has ceased. Hemodialysis is done only when there is severe, life-threatening, impairment of renal function. Disability exists when the impairment due to any chronic renal disease is expected to last 12 months with chronic hemodialysis necessitated by irreversible kidney failure. Causes of the renal failure may be hypertensive vascular disease, chronic nephritis, nephrolithiasis, polycystic disease, bilateral hydronephrosis, etc.

Hemophilia - the condition is a hereditary, sex-linked recessive trait passed from mothers to their sons. It is an abnormal tendency to bleed. Chronic inherited coagulation defects must be documented by appropriate laboratory evidence. Prophylactic therapy such as with antihemophilic globulin (AHG) concentrate does not in itself imply severity. Coagulation defects with spontaneous hemorrhage requiring transfusion at least 3 times during the 5 months prior to adjudication does constitute a disability.

Herniated Nucleus Pulposus (also known as herniated, ruptured, or prolapsed intervertebral disc; disc syndrome) - this condition is characterized by pain which is worse on movement, coughing, laughing, straining at stool, etc. There may be partial paralysis or numbness in the legs or the muscles supplied by the impaired or "pinched" nerve may become weak and wasted. Compression of the cauda equina (end of spinal cord) may cause urine retention or incontinence. Herniated nucleus pulposus may qualify as a disability when it persists for at least 3 months despite prescribed treatment and is expected to last 12 months with pain, muscle spasm, and significant limitation of motion in the spine; and appropriate radicular distribution of significant motor loss with muscle weakness and sensory and reflex loss.

Hiatal Hernia - a part of the stomach protrudes through a weak area of the diaphragm into the chest cavity. There are two main types: A. Rolling hernia-the gastroesophageal junction remains in place and the gastric cardia enters the chest cavity (more common in women). B. Sliding hernia-

(most frequent) a portion of the stomach and the gastroesophageal junction both enter the chest cavity. The condition is usually no problem if the patient sleeps with the head of the bed elevated 6 inches and takes antacids when needed. There is no cause for disability.

Hodgkin's Disease - a chronic inflammatory disease accompanied by malignant cells in the lymph nodes. Symptoms are usually unexplained fever, lymph node enlargement and intense itching. Diagnosis by biopsy and lymphangiogram are essential. There are 5 stages recognized: Stage I-the disease is limited to 1 lymph node region. Stage II-the disease involves 2 or more lymph node regions on the same side of the diaphragm. Stage III-the disease is on both sides of the diaphragm involving the lymph nodes or spleen. Stage IV -involvement outside the lymph nodes such as in the bone marrow, lungs or liver. Sub classification A-absence of constitutional symptoms. Sub classification B-the presence of constitutional symptoms of weight loss, fever, and night sweats. Sub classification E-extranodal involvement of an organ adjacent to a lymph node. For example, a patient with lung involvement would be classified as Stage II E not Stage IV. The cure rate for all stages is better than 80%. Therapy consists of a splenectomy, radiation and/ or chemotherapy. Chemotherapy is reserved for Stage III Band IV. There is cause for disability when the Hodgkin's disease becomes progressive and not controlled by prescribed therapy.

Huntington's Chorea - a dominant inherited trait characterized by involuntary movements, difficulty in speaking, unsteady gait and some degree of dementia. There is a very poor prognosis. The dementia and involuntary movements run a slow, parallel, downhill course. Suicide is common in these patients. Huntington's chorea may qualify for disability with: disorganization of motor function (significant and persistent disorganization of motor function in 2 extremities resulting in sustained disturbance of gross and dexterous movements, or gait or station); or unsteady, broad based or ataxic gait causing significant restriction of mobility substantiated by appropriate posterior column signs; or chronic brain syndrome. (See Chronic Brain Syndrome.)

Hydradenitis - inflammation of a sweat gland. A disability exists with extensive lesions under the arms or on the perineum not responding to prescribed treatment and not conducive to surgical treatment.

Hydronephrosis - formation of a cyst in the kidney due to obstruction of outflow tubes. A. Bilateral-involves both kidneys. B. Unilateral-involves one kidney. Acute hydronephrosis is usually manifested by severe pain while chronic patients may be asymptomatic or have bouts of dull flank pain. Both are usually accompanied by hematuria, fever, pyuria (pus in the urine due to infection), kidney stones (in chronic cases) and vague gastrointestinal symptoms. The definitive treatment for primary hydronephrosis is surgery and the prognosis is good. Prognosis is guarded for secondary hydronephrosis. Disability due to secondary hydronephrosis is based upon the degree of impairment in kidney function and/ or the primary disease.

Hyperglycemia - an increase above normal limits of blood sugar. Normal is 60-100 mg per 100 cc of blood. In the aged, it is 70-120 mg per 100 cc of blood. The earliest symptom is polyuria then thirst, hunger, blurred vision, nonhealing sores and weight loss. This condition is also known as diabetes mellitus. (See Diabetes Mellitus.)

Hyperparathyroidism - a condition that exists when there is an oversecretion of parathyroid hormone. There is decalcification of bones, weakness, loss of muscle tone, kidney stones, etc. There is a disability when there is generalized decalcification of bone on x-ray and an elevation of plasma calcium to 11 mg per 100 cc or greater; or a resulting impairment. Evaluate according to the criteria in the affected body system.

Hypertension - high blood pressure; generally over 140/90. Factors which may predispose one to hypertension are obesity, age, race (blacks are more likely to have and in more serious form), inheritance and oral contraceptives. Hypertension in itself is not a disability, but leads to disability when arteriosclerosis, atherosclerosis, kidney damage, heart damage, decreased blood flow to the brain or visual impairment, etc., develop.

Hypertensive Vascular Disease - refers to any disease or condition that affects the blood vessels and is related to hypertension. Two important ones are arteriosclerosis and atherosclerosis. Disability is in accordance with the body part or system affected.

Hypoparathyroidism - a condition caused by a deficiency of parathyroid hormone usually following accidental removal of or damage to the parathyroids during thyroid or other throat surgery. It is characterized by tetany, impairment of breathing, cataracts, and papilledema. There may be disability if there is severe recurrent tetany; or lenticular cataracts.

Intestinal Obstruction - A. Partial-the intestine is only partially blocked, and if treated in time, will usually open up without surgery. B. Complete-the intestine is totally blocked and must be opened quickly or gangrene will set in. C. Recurrent-the patient has a history of recurring obstructions either partial or total. These obstructions can be managed medically many times and where surgery is indicated, prognosis is usually good. An obstruction is not cause for disability unless it becomes recurrent and is unresponsive to treatment.

Kidney Transplant - a kidney taken from a donor and placed in the recipient in hopes that some kidney function may be restored. There is a disability when there is impairment of renal function due to chronic kidney disease expected to last 12 months and transplant is the alternative. The patient is considered under disability for 12 months following surgery; thereafter, evaluate for residual impairment.

Kyphoscoliosis - curvature of the spine which is angular or lateral in the thoracic region of the spine. Kyphoscoliosis may crowd the lungs to the extent that there is a restrictive ventilary disorder with total vital capacity equal to, or less than, values specified by the Social Security Administration corresponding to a person's height (Disability).

Kyphosis - curvature in the thoracic (upper) region of the spine. Usually kyphosis is not cause for disability unless there is documented functional loss.

Leukemia - a disorderly, diffuse, cancer-like growth of a particular white blood cell in the hematopoietic organs, with infiltration of the liver, spleen, kidneys, skin and other tissues. A. Acute leukemia-a disease of early life that is rapidly fatal, lasting from a few days to a few weeks. B. Chronic leukemia-often shows remissions. 1. Chronic myelogenous leukemia-affects males more than females and is most common between the ages of 20-40. It is characterized by abnormal granular leukocytes in the blood. 2. Chronic lymphatic leukemia-more often in males between 45-60. Lymphocytes are greatly increased. The first sign is generalized enlargement of lymph nodes. Acute leukemia may be considered under a disability for 2-1/2 years from the time of initial diagnosis. The diagnosis must be based upon definitive bone marrow findings. Chronic leukemia may be documented by peripheral blood bone marrow, or cerebrospinal fluid pathological findings. In addition: the patient must require one or more blood transfusions on an average of once every 2 months or at least one spontaneous hemorrhage, requiring transfusion, within 5 months prior to adjudication; or documented recurrent systemic bacterial infections occurring at least 3 times in the 5 months prior to adjudication; or non-Hodgkin's lymphoma with progressive disease not controlled by prescribed therapy.

Liver Disease - A. Chronic liver disease-any long term disease or disorder of the liver. B. Portal system-pertaining to the portal vein which brings blood to the liver along with the hepatic artery. C. Post necrotic cirrhosis-usually follows hepatitis or other inflammation and is characterized by nodules of varying sizes in the liver. D. Biliary cirrhosis-scar tissue which has developed around the bile ducts. The disease may last 1-2 years and may terminate at any time with convulsions and coma. E. Hepatitis-injury to liver cells as a result of a viral infection or toxin. 1. Acute-onset is rapid and may last from 6-8 weeks but the patient will recover if treated. 2. Chronic-long term; noninfectious with cirrhosis developing in varying degrees. See the entry on Cirrhosis for criteria for disability which covers all of these liver disorders.

Lordosis - curvature of the spine in the lumbar region. Lordosis is not cause for disability unless it can be documented that there is loss of function.

Lumbar Disc Disease - refers to disease of the discs ("cushions" of cartilage between vertebrae} in the lumbar region of the spine. A ruptured disc (herniated nucleus pulposus} is characterized by motor weakness, loss of reflex, loss of sensation, localized tenderness over the injured disc, pain, and the onset is usually 2-24 hours after the injury. See Herniated Nucleus Pulposus for disability criteria.

Lung Cancer (Pulmonary Neoplasm or Malignancy) - may be either: A. Primary-arising in the lung. B. Secondary-metastasis from other organs. Three main tissue types of lung cancer predominate: 1. Squamous cell carcinoma-made up of flat, epithelial cells (strongly linked to cigarette smoking). 2. Adenocarcinoma-a metastasis spread through the blood stream. 3. Undifferentiated forms-oat cell carcinoma.

The treatment of choice is surgical resection when possible, then radiation or chemotherapy. Cancer of the lungs qualifies for a disability when it is unresectable; or with metastasis, or recurrent after resection; or incomplete incision; or oat cell carcinoma (fast spreading and difficult even to slow its progression, and is impossible to cure).

Lung Infection (Mycotic) - a lung infection caused by a microorganism. There is disability when there is a culture of specific organisms, x-ray evidence, evidence of the condition persisting for 3 months despite prescribed therapy; or a culture of specific organisms from sputa and current x-ray evidence of a lesion and episodes of hemoptysis occurring at least once every 2 months; or impairment of pulmonary function due to extensive disease. Lupus - a skin disease. A. Lupus erythematosus-inflammation of the skin with scaly patches. B. Scleroderma-a condition characterized by hardening and thickening of the skin; occasionally pigmented and stiff. C. Disseminated lupus-lupus affecting the whole system. Disseminated lupus erythematosus is cause for disability when it is established by a positive LE preparation or a biopsy or a positive ANA test with frequent symptoms demonstrating involvement of the renal or the cardiac or the pulmonary or the gastrointestinal or the central nervous systems. There is a disability with scleroderma or progressive systemic sclerosis (the diffuse or generalized form) with advanced limitation of use of the hands due to sclerodactylia (affecting the fingers) or limitation in other joints; or significant visceral manifestations of digestive, cardiac, or pulmonary impairment.

Malabsorption - a disorder wherein nutrients are not absorbed by the blood from the villi of the small intestines in the volume needed for good health. In itself malabsorption is not a disability unless there is significant weight loss or some deficiency disease. Then it would be evaluated under the specific problem for disability. Malabsorption of fats leads to a deficiency of Vitamins A, D and K which may result in tetany, muscle cramps, bone pain, pathological fractures of ribs and vertebrae, osteoporosis, hypoalbuminuria, peripheral edema, anemia or coagulation defects. Malabsorption of iron, folic acid, or Vitamin Bl2 may produce fatigue, dyspnea, weakness, low blood pressure, abdominal distention with hyperactive bowel sounds.

Malassimilation - a disorder wherein the body cannot assimilate certain substances from the food eaten. Disability would be evaluated according to the specific resulting disorder. The range of symptoms and impairments are very similar to those listed for Malabsorption.

Malignancy of the Abdomen - cancer affecting any part of the abdomen. There is cause for disability when there is generalized carcinoma; or retroperitoneal cellular sarcoma not controlled by prescribed therapy; or ascites with demonstrated malignant cells.

Malignancy of the Brain or Spinal Cord - cancer. There is disability when there is metastatic carcinoma to the brain or spinal cord; or they are malignant gliomas; or there is disorganization of motor function.

Malignancy of the Esophagus or Stomach - cancer. Criteria for disability are carcinoma or sarcoma of the upper two-thirds of the esophagus; or carcinoma or sarcoma of the distal one-third of the esophagus with metastasis to the regional lymph nodes or extension to surrounding structures; or carcinoma of the stomach with metastasis to the regional lymph nodes or extension to surrounding structures; or sarcoma of the stomach not controlled by prescribed therapy; or inoperable carcinoma; or recurrence or metastasis after resection.

Malignancy of the Kidneys, Adrenal Glands, or Ureters
- cancer. Criteria for disability are carcinoma that is
unresectable; or with metastasis.

**Malignancy of the Large Intestine (from ileocecal valve
to and including anal canal)** - Criteria for disability are
carcinoma or sarcoma that is unresectable; or metastasis
beyond the regional lymph nodes; or recurrence or
metastasis after resection.

Malignancy of the Liver or Gallbladder - cancer. Criteria
for disability are primary or metastatic malignant tumors of
the liver, or carcinoma of the gallbladder; or carcinoma of
the bile ducts, unresectable or with metastasis.

Malignancy of Lymph Nodes - cancer. There is a
disability when there is Hodgkin's disease or non-Hodgkin's
lymphoma with progressive disease not controlled by
prescribed therapy; or metastatic carcinoma in a lymph
node (except for epidermoid carcinoma in a lymph node in
the neck) where the primary site is not determined after
adequate search; or epidermoid carcinoma in a lymph node
in the neck that is not responding to prescribed therapy.

**Malignancy of the Mandible, Maxilla, Orbit or
Temporal Fossa** A. Mandible-the lower jawbone. B.
Maxilla-the upper jawbone. C. Orbit-the bony cavity in the
skull that holds the eyeballs. D. Temporal fossa-the shallow
depressions on the sides of the skull at the temples. The
criteria for disability are sarcoma of any type with
metastasis; or carcinoma of the antrum (inner part of skull)
with extension into the orbit or ethmoid or sphenoid sinus,
or with regional or distant metastasis; or orbital tumors

with intracranial extension; or tumors of the temporal fossa with perforation of skull and meningeal involvement; or adamantinoma with orbital or intracranial infiltration; or tumors of Rathke's pouch with infiltration of the base of the skull or metastasis.

Malignancy of Pleura or Mediastinum - cancer. A. Pleura-the serous membrane that enfolds the lungs. B. Mediastinum-the space between the left and right lung. There is cause for disability when there is malignant mesothelioma of the pleura; or malignant tumors, metastatic to the pleura; or malignant primary tumor of the mediastinum not controlled by prescribed therapy.

Malignancy of Prostate Gland - cancer of prostate gland. Prostate gland is defined as a gland found in males that produces a seminal fluid. It often stops functioning in the elderly. There may be cause for disability when the carcinoma is inoperable and is not controlled by prescribed therapy.

Malignancy of Salivary Glands - cancer of the salivary glands. The salivary glands are four pairs of glands that produce saliva. A. Parotid glands-located on each side of the face below the ear which secrete ptyalin, an enzyme that begins breaking down starch while food is being chewed. B. Submaxillary glands-in the floor of the mouth. C. Sublingual glands-in the floor of the mouth and under the tongue. D. Buccal glands-scattered beneath the mucous membrane of the lips and cheek. Criteria for disability is carcinoma or sarcoma with metastasis beyond the regional lymph nodes.

Malignancy of the Skeletal System (exclusive of the jaw) or Cancer of the Bone - any persistent or progressive pain involving the trunk or the extremities, especially if associated with a mass, must be considered a bone tumor until proved otherwise. Criteria for disability is a malignant primary tumor with evidence of metastasis and not controlled by prescribed therapy; or metastatic carcinoma to bone where the primary site is not determined after adequate search.

Malignancy of the Small Intestine - cancer of the small intestine. It is most common in the ileum producing pain, obstruction, bleeding, and rapid weight loss. Most carcinoid tumors are not invasive; therefore, the prognosis is good in most cases. The criteria for disability is carcinoma, sarcoma, or carcinoid tumor with metastasis beyond the regional lymph nodes; or recurrence of carcinoma, sarcoma or carcinoid tumor after resection; or sarcoma, not controlled by prescribed therapy.

Malignancy of the Thyroid Gland - cancer of the thyroid glands. Thyroid glands are endocrine glands located in the neck which produce hormones that control growth and metabolism. The patient usually becomes aware of a mass or "lump" in the neck that is not painful or tender. Disability may exist when there is carcinoma with metastasis beyond the regional lymph nodes not controlled by prescribed therapy.

Malignant Glioma - cancer of nervous tissue. A. Astrocytoma-tumor formed of star-shaped cells in the nervous system. B. Glioblastoma-cancer of the central nervous system, especially the cerebellum (part of the brain). C. Medulloblastoma-a malignant tumor of nerve tissue in bone marrow. D. Ependymoblastoma-a cancer of the membrane lining the central canal of the spinal cord. See Brain Tumors, Tumors of the Back, Malignancy of the Brain or Spinal Cord.

Malignant Melanoma - a malignant tumor that may arise anywhere the color pigment melanin (skin, mucous membranes, eye) is found. There are three major types, but all have one factor in common; they spread rapidly and death occurs within months. 1. Lentigo Maligna Melanoma-arises from a large freckle on the face or other sun-exposed parts in elderly people. It is a flat, tan or brown spot with darker brown or black spots scattered irregularly over the surface. 2. Superficial Spreading Melanoma-usually occurs on the legs in women and on the torso of men. This is the most common type. It appears as an enlarged, discolored, lesion with raised edges and it may have red, white, blue, or blue-black nodules. 3. Nodular Melanoma-may occur anywhere on the body and at almost any age. It is a dark, elevated area that rapidly enlarges. The criteria for disability is that the disease is widespread after wide excision; or with metastasis to adjacent tissue or elsewhere.

Malnutrition/Weight Loss - a diagnosed primary disorder of the digestive tract that interferes with nutrition and results in weight loss. These disorders are: enterocolitis, chronic pancreatitis, post gastrointestinal resection, or esophageal stricture, stenosis or obstruction. A disability exists when the weight corresponds to certain established values and a serum albumin of 3.0 gm per 100 cc or less; or a hematocrit of 30% or less, or serum calcium of 8.0 mg per 100 cc or less; or uncontrolled diabetes mellitus; or fat in stool of 7 gm or greater per 24-hour specimen; or persistent or recurrent ascites or edema not attributable to other causes.

Meniere's Disease - a combination of tinnitus, vertigo, and deafness. These disturbances of balance may be constant or intermittent attacks with nausea, vomiting, ataxia, and incapacitation. Prognosis is variable because remission in chronic cases varies. Surgical treatment has good results, while streptomycin therapy may cause injury to the cochlea. There may be a disability when there is a history of frequent attacks of balance disturbance, tinnitus, and a progressive loss of hearing with disturbed function of the vestibular labyrinth demonstrated by caloric or other vestibular tests; and hearing loss established by audiometry.

Mental Retardation - IQ of 69 or less marked by severe mental and social incapacity and a dependence on others for personal needs. There is a disability when manifested by severe mental and social incapacity as evidenced by marked dependence upon others for personal needs (e.g., bathing, washing, dressing, etc.) and the inability to understand spoken words and the inability to follow simple direction and the inability to read, write, and perform simple calculations; or IQ of 59 or less; or IQ of 60-69 inclusive with a physical or other mental impairment imposing additional and significant work-related limitation of function.

Multiform Bullosum - a skin disease with multiple lesions. It may be a cause for disability if accompanied by extensive lesions that do not respond to prescribed treatment.

Multiple Sclerosis (MS) - a progressive, chronic hardening of the nervous system and a chronic thickening of the arteries. There may be a disability with disorganization of motor function (significant and persistent disorganization of motor function in 2 extremities, resulting in sustained disturbances of gross and dexterous movements, or gait and station); or visual or mental impairment.

Myasthenia Gravis - generalized muscular weakness without atrophy. The end fibers of nerve tissue fail to transform impulse into action. The disease is usually improved with cholinesterase-inhibiting drugs. The onset may be sudden or gradual. The first symptom is usually a drooping eyelid, followed by difficulty in swallowing, difficulty in moving joints, limb weakness and respiratory difficulty which is potentially life threatening. Thyroid disorders are frequently concurrent with myasthenia gravis. The criteria for disability is significant difficulty with speaking, swallowing, or breathing while on prescribed therapy; or significant motor weakness of the muscles of the extremities or repetitive activity against resistance while on prescribed therapy.

Myelofibrosis (Myeloproliferative Syndrome) - a progressive disease in which bone marrow is replaced by fibrous tissue causing anemia, hepatomegaly and splenomegaly. There is a disability with chronic anemia (see the entry on anemia); or documented recurrent systemic bacterial infections occurring at least 3 times during the 5 months prior to adjudication; or intractable bone pain with radiologic evidence of osteosclerosis.

Myocardial Infarction (Acute) (also known as "heart attack") - injury and death of heart muscle due to an insufficient blood supply when one or more of the coronary arteries are obstructed. The patient usually complains of crushing chest pain which radiates to the upper stomach, neck, jaw, and arms. Other symptoms may be sweating, nausea, weakness, and anxiety.

With appropriate medical care the overall prognosis is good. Prognosis is dependent upon the length of time between the onset of pain and treatment, the extent and location of myocardial damage and the development of complications. Some important complications are congestive heart failure, ventricular aneurysm and ventricular fibrillation. Myocardial infarction (acute) is classified as ischemic heart disease by the Social Security Administration. The criteria for disability is: A. Treadmill exercise demonstrating one of the following at an exercise level of 5 METS or less: 1. Horizontal or down-sloping ischemic depression of the ST segment to 1.0 mm or greater, clearly discernible in at least 2 consecutive complexes which are on a level baseline in any lead; or 2. Premature ventricular systoles which are multiform or bidirectional or are sequentially inscribed (3 or more); or 3. ST segment elevation to 3 mm or greater; or 4. Development of second- or third-degree heart block; or B. In the absence of a report of an acceptable treadmill exercise test, one of the following: 1. Transmural myocardial infarction exhibiting a QS pattern or a Q wave with amplitude at least 1/3 of R wave and with a duration of 0.04 second or more. (If these are present in leads III and a VF only, the requisite Q wave findings must be shown, by labelled tracing, to persist on deep inspiration; or 2. Resting ECG findings showing ischemic-type (original copy) depression of ST segment to more than 0.5 mm in either leads land a VL and V, or leads II and III and a VF or leads V3 through V6; or 3. Resting EKG findings showing an ischemic configuration or current of injury with ST segment elevation to 2 mm or more in either leads I and a VL and V6 or leads II and III and a VF or leads V3 through V6; or 4. Resting EKG findings showing symmetrical inversion of T waves to 5.0 mm or more in any two leads except III or a VR or V, or V2; or 5. Inversion of T waves to 1.0 mm or more in any of leads I, II, a VL, V2 to V4 and R waves greater than S wave in lead a VF; or 6. "Double" Master two-step test demonstrating one of the following: (a) Ischemic depression ST segment to more than 0.5 mm lasting for at least 0.08 second beyond the J junction and clearly discernible in at least 2 consecutive complexes which are on a level baseline in any lead; or (b) Development of a second- or third-degree heart block; or 7. Angiographic evidence (obtained independent of the Social Security disability evaluation) showing one of the following: (a) 50% or more narrowing of the left main coronary artery; or (b) 70% or more narrowing of a proximal coronary artery (excluding the left main coronary artery); or (c) 50% or more narrowing involving a long (greater than 1 cm) segment of a proximal coronary artery or multiple proximal coronary arteries; or C. Resting E KG findings showing left bundle branch block as evidenced by QRS duration of 0.12 second or more in leads I, II, or III and R peak duration of 0.06 second or more in leads I, a VL, V 5 or V 6, unless there is a coronary angiogram of record which is negative; or D. Left ventricular ejection fraction of 30% or less measured at cardiac catheterization or by echocardiography.

Myocardial Ischemia and Angina Pectoris - A. Myocardial ischemia is the condition caused by an imbalance between myocardial oxygen supply and demand. B. Angina pectoris is the pain, fullness and heaviness caused by myocardial ischemia, brought on by exertion or excitement, and usually relieved by nitroglycerine. For those patients with 80% obstruction in at least 2 main arteries; aortocoronary bypass surgery is indicated. Bypass surgery most often relieves all symptoms of angina. In other cases, prognosis depends upon the patient's general health. For disability criteria see the entry on Myocardial Infarction and Chest Pain of Cardiac Origin. Myocardiopathies (Cardiomyopathies) - a disease that affects the heart muscle. It may be primary or secondary. Primary myocardiopathies are those characterized by changes in the myocardial structure and function which cannot be attributed to a specific cause. Secondary myocardiopathies are dysfunctions associated with other diseases. Disability is based upon the particular disease or condition and the degree of impairment associated with it.

Myotonic Dystrophy - a hereditary weakness of many of the major muscles of the body. There is a progression of muscle-wasting with death in the early 60's in the majority of cases. There is a disability when there is a loss of major function due to degenerative changes in association with loss of muscle mass in both hands; or both feet; or one hand and one foot; or disorganization of motor function. Cardiac arrhythmia may develop with myotonic dystrophy, and if it does, disability may be based upon that evidence as well.

Nephrotic Syndrome - a set of symptoms such as excessive excretion of protein in the urine, less albumin than is normal, and edema. The symptoms are anorexia, weakness, fatigue, edema, and sometimes hypertension. There is a disability for nephrotic syndrome when there is anasarca, persistent for at least 3 months despite prescribed therapy with a serum albumin of 3.0 gm per 100 cc or less and a proteinuria of 3.5 gm per 24 hours or greater ; or proteinuria of 10.0 gm per 24 hours or greater.

Neurohypophyseal Insufficiency (Diabetes Insipidus) (also known as Polyuria) - an enormous urine output that is very often the result of a tumor of the pituitary gland or ahead injury or it may be a congenital, inherited condition. There are two kinds recognized: A. Nephrogenic diabetes insipidus-an inherited recessive trait affecting males. There is polyuria and extreme thirst. B. Vasopressin-sensitive diabetes insipidus-usually the result of a tumor of or an injury to the pituitary gland which causes the gland to discontinue its production of vasopressin (ADH) hormone that concentrates the urine. Dehydration is a very real and dangerous complication to both kinds. Both usually respond to medical treatment except in the case of operable tumors of the pituitary. There may be a disability with a urine specific gravity of 1.005 or below, persistent for at least 3 months and recurrent dehydration.

Neurosis (Functional Non-Psychotic Disorders) - defects in the personality most often involving the perception of and reaction to stressful situations. The main types are: A. Anxiety-a functional mental disturbance caused by fear. B. Depressive neurosis-bouts of self-doubt, self-criticism, hopelessness, and lack of mental and physical energy. C. Obsessive-compulsive-an uncontrolled desire to do something or to dwell on a thought or idea. D. Phobia-unusual fears of situations or objects. E. Hysteria-an attitude of indifference toward involuntary muscular movements or paralysis. F. Hypochondria-an unusual preoccupation with imagined diseases or disorders of one's body. These are considered under functional non-psychotic disorders. For disability, the neurosis must demonstrate findings from both A and B: A. Manifested persistence of one or more of the following clinical signs: 1. Demonstrable and persistent structural changes mediated through psychophysiological channels (e.g., duodenal ulcer); or 2. Recurrent and persistent periods of anxiety, with tension, apprehension and interference with concentration and memory; or 3. Persistent depressive affect with insomnia, loss of weight and suicidal thoughts; or 4. Persistent phobic or obsessive ruminations with inappropriate, bizarre or disruptive behavior; or 5. Persistent, compulsive, ritualistic behavior; or 6. Persistent functional disturbance of vision, speech, hearing or use of a limb with demonstrable structural or trophic changes; or 7. Persistent, deeply ingrained, maladaptive patterns of behavior manifested by either: (a) Seclusiveness or autistic thinking; or (b) Pathologically inappropriate suspiciousness or hostility; or B. Resulting persistence of marked restriction of daily activities and constriction of interests and deterioration in personal habits and seriously impaired ability to relate to other people.

Obesity - overweight. Obesity in itself is not a disability unless it is equal to or greater than the values specified by the Social Security Administration and one of the following: a history of pain and limitation of motion in every weight-bearing joint or spine (or physical exam) associated with x-ray evidence of arthritis in weight-bearing joints or the spine; or hypertension with diastolic blood pressure persistently in excess of 100 mm of mercury (Hg) measured with appropriate size cuff; or history of CHF manifested by past evidence of vascular congestion such as hepatomegaly, peripheral or pulmonary edema; or chronic venous insufficiency with superficial varicose veins in a lower extremity with pain on weight-bearing and a persistent edema; or respiratory disease with total forced vital capacity equal to or less than 2.0 Lor a level of hypoxemia at rest equal to or less than values specified by the Social Security Administration.

Obsessive-Compulsive - involves an uncontrolled desire to do something or to dwell on an idea or thought. For disability criteria, see Neurosis.

Optic Atrophy - damage to the optic nerve resulting from different causes. 1. Primary-no evidence of previous inflammation, edema, a reduced number of living optic nerve fibers, and reduced blood supply to the optic disc. 2. Secondary-disc margins are blurred and glial overgrowth are observed. There is decreased central or peripheral vision, as this is an end stage and the damage is permanent. There is a disability for impairment of central visual acuity when remaining vision in the better eye after best correction is 20/200 or less; or contraction of peripheral visual field in the better eye to 10¡ or less from the point of fixation; or so the widest diameter subtends an angle no greater than 20¡; or to 20% or less visual field efficiency.

Osteitis Fibrosa - a disease in which fibrous tissue replaces bony tissue. This is usually associated with a disorder of the parathyroid in which calcium is extracted from the bones and is deposited in the kidneys causing them to harden (hyperparathyroidism). See Hyperparathyroidism.

Osteomyelitis - an infection of the bone or bone marrow most frequently caused by Staphylococcus aureus. The prognosis is excellent if treatment is begun in time. There may be cause for disability if it persists with at least 2 episodes within a 5-month period and x-ray shows that it exists in the pelvis, vertebrae, femur, tibia, or a major joint of an upper or lower extremity. There also should be laboratory findings of leukocytosis and an elevated sedimentation rate.

Osteoporosis - softening of bones due to calcium phosphate being withdrawn. This is particularly significant among menopausal and postmenopausal women. There is a disability if generalized osteoporosis is established by x-ray, manifested by pain and limitation of back motion and paravertebral muscle spasms with x-ray evidence of either compression fractures of vertebrae; or other disorders (e.g., herniated nucleus pulposus or spinal stenosis) and with pain, muscle spasm, significant limitation of motion in the spine; weakness and sensory and reflex loss persisting for at least 3 months and expected to last 12 months in spite of pre- scribed therapy.

Osteosclerosis - a progressive disease wherein the bones become harder and heavier. Other names are Albers-Schonberg disease, marble bones, osteitis, osteopetrosis, osteopoikilosis, and Paget's disease. This disease develops slowly and usually without symptoms. It is discovered when x-rays or an elevated alkaline phosphatase (blood test) is done for some other purpose. The most commonly affected bones are, in order, the pelvis, femur, skull, tibia, vertebrae, clavicle (collar bone), and humerus (upper arm). The course of the disease is slowly progressive causing deformity, joint immobility and spinal compression. A disability would be evaluated by the criteria for the impairment of the body system most affected.

Otosclerosis - a hereditary disease of the bones of the middle ear. It is more common in females. Surgical repair restores some degree of hearing. A late postoperative complication is perilymph fistula (sudden decrease in hearing) and should be treated as an emergency. A disability may exist when hearing impairment is properly documented and hearing is not restorable by a hearing aid and manifested by: average hearing threshold sensitivity for air conduction of 90 decibels or greater, and for bone conduction to corresponding maximal levels, in the better ear, determined by the simple average of hearing threshold levels at 500, 1000 and 200 hz.; or speech discrimination scores of 40% or less in the better ear.

Ovarian Tumors - 30-40% of ovarian tumors are malignant and are rarely detected until late in the course of the disease. Treatment depends on the pathological diagnosis and the degree of invasion into the surrounding tissue. For malignant tumors, surgery, radiation therapy and/ or chemotherapy are the advised treatment. When the tumors are benign, the prognosis is excellent; but malignant tumors of the ovary have a poor prognosis. They are the fourth leading cause of death in American females. There is no disability unless it is malignant, and inoperable; or recurrent and with metastasis.

Pancreatic Dysfunction - any disease, lesion or disorder that prevents the pancreas from functioning normally. The most common result is diabetes mellitus. See Diabetes Mellitus for disability.

Parkinson's Disease - a chronic disease of the nervous system characterized by tremor, muscular weakness and sclerosis and a peculiar gait. Parkinson's syndrome is chronic and progressive even with therapy. The patient may eventually become unable to care for himself. With the best medical attention, patients usually remain functional for 10-20 years. Mental deterioration is not seen until late in the course of the disease. Parkinson's disease or syndrome qualifies under a disability with the following signs: significant rigidity, bradykinesia, or tremor in two extremities, which, singly or in combination, result in sustained disturbance of gross and dexterous movements, or gait or station.

Paroxysmal Supraventricular Tachycardia - a very fast atrial heartbeat that is changing and recurrent in nature. Heart rate is 140-250 beats per minute. This usually occurs first during youth and is usually seen in patients with no organic heart disease. Treatment consists of carotid massage, rest, mild sedation, reassurance, vasopressor agents if hypertensive, electrical cardioversion, cardiac glycoside or cholinesterase inhibitor. For frequent or long-lasting attacks treatment consist of digitalis, procainamide, quinidine or propanolol. The patient should avoid fatigue, coffee, tea, alcohol, and tobacco. The prognosis is excellent in most cases. See Arrhythmia for disability.

Pelvic Fracture - a break in one or more of the pelvic bones. These fractures may be stable or unstable and soft tissue injury can be serious. Most fractures are named according to the pelvic bone involved. General kinds are: A. Avulsion fracture-the forcible tearing away of a structure or part (quite common in motorcycle accidents). B. Malgaigne fracture-type of fracture in which the bone breaks through one set of public rami and the region of the sacroiliac joint. This is an unstable fracture. C. Stellate fracture-a fracture with several breaks or cracks radiating from a central point of injury. (A stellate fracture of the ileum has a temporary disability of 8-12 weeks). A ruptured bladder, a perforated colon, and laceration of blood vessels are of primary concern and must be treated promptly. Prognosis depends on the type of fracture and associated injury to internal organs. The main complications are: bladder injury, rupture and severing of the urethra, hemorrhage, thrombophlebitis and embolism, and sciatic nerve damage. The emboli are usually pulmonary, but may be cerebral or renal and cause sudden death or permanent damage. There is cause for disability as the result of a pelvic fracture with solid union not evident on x-ray and not clinically solid, when such determination is feasible, and return to full weightbearing status did not occur or is not expected to occur within 12 months of onset.

Pelvic Relaxation - a condition resulting from childbirth in which the uterus and bladder become displaced from their normal positions. Surgery is the definitive treatment. The prognosis depends upon the surgeon's skill. There is no cause for disability.

Pemphigus - a rare skin disorder characterized by blisters which affects apparently healthy skin and mucous membranes. Pemphigus foliaceus is usually benign and responds well to treatment, but both pemphigus vulgaris and pemphigus vegetans are slowly progressive, debilitating, difficult to treat, and are usually fatal. It is cause for a disability when it becomes extensive and does not respond to prescribed treatment.

Peptic Ulcer - an open lesion of the mucous lining of the duodenum or stomach. There are several types recognized: 1. Duodenal ulcer-a peptic ulcer in the duodenum, usually in the first few centimeters. 2. Gastric ulcer-occurs along the lesser curvature of the stomach. 3. Channel ulcer-occurs in the pyloric canal. 4. Post bulbar-a peptic ulcer in Meckel's diverticulum. 5. Marginal or stomal-peptic ulcer at the margin of the anastomosis (where the stomach and small intestine join). 6. Jejunal ulcer-a peptic ulcer found in the jejunum. Duodenal and gastric ulcers are the most common types. With proper therapy, symptoms are relieved in just a few days and with continued prescribed therapy the healing process is completed. See Gastrectomy for criteria for disability in cases of chronic peptic ulcer disease.

Peripheral Neuropathies - any disease of nervous tissue other than the central nervous system (made up of the brain and spinal cord) with sensory, motor, reflex and vasomotor symptoms. 1. Mononeuropathy or mononeuritis-disease of one nerve. 2. Mononeuritis multiplex-disease of 2 or more nerves in separate places. 3. Polyneuropathy, polyneuritis or multiple peripheral neuritis-disease of many nerves at the same time. Both single and multiplex mononeuritis are marked by pain, weakness, partial paralysis and they are asymmetric. Polyneuropathy is bilaterally symmetrical, most commonly seen with diabetes mellitus or malnutrition and it develops slowly. The patient has peripheral tingling, numbness, burning pain (the pain is worse at night), sensory loss, loss of reflexes, painless ulcers on the digits, weakness, atrophy, hyperemia, sweating, bullae, pallor, dry skin and osteoporosis. There may be a cause for disability when there is disorganization of function in spite of prescribed therapy.

Perirectal Suppuration - an abscess in the anus that may affect the surrounding tissue. This condition is painful, but prognosis is excellent with proper treatment. In the case of rare supralevator abscess, peritonitis or a fistula in ano may result. There is usually no cause for disability unless there is an intermittent obstruction due to an intractable abscess or formation of a fistula in ano.

Peritoneal Dialysis - the patient's own peritoneum is used as a dialysis filter when chronic kidney failure begins. There are many things to consider: the patient's discomfort during the procedure, hemorrhage around the puncture site, perforation of some abdominal structure, fluid in the chest cavity, protein loss, coma, low blood pressure and peritonitis. Impairment of renal function due to any chronic kidney disease expected to last 12 months with chronic hemodialysis or peritoneal dialysis necessitated by irreversible renal failure is cause for disability.

Peritonitis (Acute) - an inflammation of the peritoneum usually caused by bacteria but may be due to chemical or mechanical stimuli. Localized peritonitis frequently occurs in diverticulitis or early appendicitis, while a ruptured appendix or a perforated ulcer or perforated colon from carcinoma or leakage of bile may cause widespread peritonitis. Symptoms are pain, nausea and vomiting, occasionally diarrhea, fever, chills, tenderness, distention, tachycardia, elevated leukocyte count. All or part of the symptoms may appear. If it is untreated, it may be fatal, but it is not a disability.

Persistent Disorganization of Motor Function - in two extremities, resulting in sustained disturbance of gross and dexterous movements, or gait and station. Disorganization of motor function in the form of paresis or paralysis, ataxia and sensory disturbances (any or all of which may be due to cerebral, cerebellar, brain stem, spinal cord, or peripheral nerve dysfunction) which occur singly or in various combinations, frequently provides the sole or partial basis for decision in cases of neurological impairment. The assessment of impairment depends upon the degree of interference with locomotion and/ or interference with the use of fingers, hands, and arms.

Pleural Effusion - fluid around the lungs in the pleural cavity caused by various infections, TB, pneumonia, rheumatic fever, an abscess, cancer, etc. Treatment is based on an analysis of the effusion. Prognosis depends upon the underlying cause of the effusion. Pleural effusion is not cause for a disability, but the underlying cause may be.

Pneumoconiosis - a condition of the respiratory tract that develops after prolonged inhalation of dust-of any kind. A. Fibrogenic pneumoconiosis or silicosis-caused by inhaling free silica resulting in pulmonary fibrosis. B. Black lung disease {also known as coal worker's pneumoconiosis, coal miner's pneumoconiosis and anthracosis) -coal dust is deposited throughout the lungs as a result of long-term exposure. C. Asbestosis-fibrous pneumoconiosis that results from inhalation of asbestos fibers. D. Chemical pneumoconiosis-results from long-term inhalation of irritant chemical gases and vapors which damages the bronchial mucosa and lung tissue. Pneumoconiosis is cause for disability as demonstrated by x-ray with nodular or focal fibrosis {nonconglomerative); spirometric evidence of chronic airway obstruction demonstrated by MVV and FEV; or interstitial or disseminated fibrosis or conglomerative disease.

Polyarteritis {also known as polyarteritis nodosa, periarteritis nodosa, and necrotizing angiitis) - a disease of small and medium sized arteries in which there is localized necrosis and inflammation with ischemia of the tissue supplied by the arteries. The most common complaints are fever, abdominal pain, weakness, asthma, hypertension, edema, nausea, vomiting, diarrhea, infrequent urination, headache, convulsions, etc. This disease mimics many other disorders; therefore, tests should be done as a possible diagnosis for unexplained combinations of the above symptoms. Whether acute or chronic, the disease usually causes death because it leads to failure of the heart, kidneys and/or other vital organs. Renal failure due to polyarteritis is the leading cause of death in this category. Prognosis is very poor even with proper treatment. Disability is considered based upon the organ or system that is impaired.

Polycystic Kidney Disease - a congenital, bilateral kidney disease in which there is gradual replacement of renal tissue by cyst-like structures.

Most patients die of complications due to hypertension or cerebral aneurysm within 10 years of the onset. Criteria for disability are impairment of renal function due to chronic polycystic disease expected to last 12 months with chronic hemodialysis or peritoneal dialysis necessitated by irreversible renal failure; or persistent elevation of serum creatinine to 4 mg per 100 cc or greater or reduction of creatinine clearance to 10 ml per minute (29 liters per 24 hours) or less, over at least 3 months with one of the following: 1. Renal osteodystrophy manifested by severe bone pain and appropriate x-ray abnormalities (e.g., osteitis, fibrosis, severe osteoporosis, pathologic fractures);

or 2. Persistent motor or sensory neuropathy; or 3. A clinical episode of pericarditis; or 4. Intractable pruritus; or 5. Persistent fluid overload syndrome resulting in diastolic hypertension (110 mm or above) or signs of vascular congestion; or 6. Persistent anorexia with weight loss; or 7. Persistent hematocrits of 30% or less.

Polycythemia Vera (also known as Erythrocytosis) - an excess of red blood cells. The excess of red blood cells results in an increased amount or volume of blood as well as thicker than normal blood, both of which cause impaired blood flow and causes the heart to work extra hard to pump the increased volume of thick blood. Some symptoms are fatigue, headache, drowsiness, difficulty in concentration, forgetfulness and vertigo. Treatment reduces symptoms and places the patient in remission for 5-10 years. Death is usually due to complications of myelofibrosis, acute of esophageal varices with a documented history of massive hemorrhage attributable to those varices; or performance of a shunt operation for esophageal varices; or serum bilirubin leukemia, etc. Disability is evaluated under the body system affected. For example, Myelofibrosis or Acute Leukemia.

Portal Hypertension - congestion in the liver and spleen secondary to cirrhosis, thrombosis of some blood vessel in the liver, tumor, fibrosis or sclerosis. This disease usually develops silently. The patient may be an alcoholic. Underlying obstructions such as tumor or thrombosis can sometimes be corrected by surgery. Early therapy of cirrhosis can prevent portal hypertension; however, cirrhosis is irreversible. Total abstention from alcohol is the only means of slowing down the process. The criteria for disability is documentation of portal hypertension with x-ray or endoscopic evidence of 2.5 mg per 100 cc or greater persisting on repeated examinations for at least 5 months; or hepatic coma; or confirmation of chronic liver disease by liver biopsy and one of the following: 1. Ascites not attributable to other causes, recurring or persisting for at least 3 months, demonstrated by abdominal paracentesis or associated with persistent hypoalbuminemia of 3.0 gm per 100 cc or less. 2. Serum bilirubin of 2.5 mg per cc or greater on repeated examinations. 3. Hepatic cell necrosis or inflammation, persisting for at least 3 months, documented by repeated abnormalities of prothrombin time and enzymes indicative of hepatic dysfunction.

Postgastrointestinal Resection - surgical removal of a portion or all of the stomach and connecting small intestine. The dumping syndrome is a common complication. This condition is usually not cause for disability. For most patients the complications clear up with proper treatment.

Primary Dysmenorrhea - painful menstruation with no demonstrable pelvic disorder. This condition responds well to treatment and is not cause for a disability.

Psoriasis - a chronic and recurrent skin disorder characterized by scaling papules. Psoriasis varies in severity from 1 or 2 patches of dry, scaly skin to widespread manifestation with exfoliation or disabling arthritis. A. Psoriatic arthritis-very closely resembles rheumatoid arthritis and is just as disabling, but the patient does not have the rheumatoid factor in his/her blood serum. B. Exfoliative psoriatic dermatitis-very difficult to treat and may lead to disability because the entire skin is red and covered with scales. C. Pustular psoriasis-sterile pustules usually localized to the palms of the hands and soles of the feet. This may be cause for temporary or permanent disability because it is painful, difficult to treat, and may limit the use of the hands and/or feet. All forms tend to recur after remission. Psoriasis with extensive lesions, including involvement of the hands or feet which impose a severe limitation of function and which are not responding to prescribed treatment is the basis for a disability claim. Psoriatic arthritis would be evaluated as rheumatoid arthritis minus a positive blood test for the RA factor.

Psychosis - a mental disorder in which the patient is unable to adapt to the outside world. It is characterized by abnormal behavior, withdrawal from reality or disorganized thought. Psychosis may be the result of certain organic conditions such as senile or presenile dementia, intracranial infection, central nervous system degenerative disease, delirium tremens or other endocrinologic, metabolic or toxic states. These are considered functional psychotic disorders. The main types are: A. Schizophrenia (see Schizophrenia) 1. Hebephrenic 2. Catatonic 3. Paranoid. B. Senile dementia (see Senile Dementia) C. Alzheimer's disease. (see Senile Dementia) Functional psychotic disorders are evaluated for disability on the following criteria (with both A and B): A. Manifested persistence of one or more of the following clinical signs: 1. Depression or elation; or 2. Agitation; or 3. Psychomotor disturbance; or 4. Hallucinations or delusions; or 5. Autistic or other regressive behavior; or 6. Inappropriateness of affect; or 7. Illogical association of ideas. B. Resulting persistence of marked restriction of daily activities and constriction of interests and seriously impaired ability to relate to other people.

Pulmonary Embolisms - the lodging of a blood clot in the lung resulting in local obstruction of blood flow. These emboli most often arise from an existing thrombus deep in the pelvic or leg veins. Treatment consists of bed rest for 5-7 days, anticoagulants, support stockings and surgery in massive cases. Prognosis depends upon the extent of the embolism and the previous condition of the patient. Pulmonary emboli that cause acute cor pulmonale must be treated as a medical emergency. There is no cause for disability unless there is pulmonary insufficiency as a result and it can be documented by MVV and FEY.

Pulmonary Fibrosis - a disease characterized by lung tissue replacement with tough, fiber-like tissue causing pulmonary impairments. There are several kinds: A. Pneumoconiosis 1. Silicosis 2. Black lung disease 3. Asbestosis 4. Chemical pneumoconiosis. B. Cystic fibrosis-affects other systems as well. See the entries for Pneumoconiosis and Cystic Fibrosis.

Pulmonary Resection - the surgical removal of all or part of a lung. A pulmonary resection may cause restrictive ventilary disorders. There is a disability when there is a total vital capacity equal to, or less than the Social Security Administration specified values corresponding to the person's height.

Pyelonephritis (Acute) - an acute kidney infection which may be secondary to sickle cell disease, neurogenic bladder, diabetes or hypertension. Treatment consists of the appropriate antibiotic to control the bacteria causing the infection and repeated cultures to make sure it is cleared. Recovery is usually complete but it may recur. Prolonged cases may cause kidney damage, but then it is considered chronic pyelonephritis. Acute pyelonephritis in itself is not cause for disability. The underlying disease or condition may be.

Pyelonephritis (Chronic) - a chronic, bilateral, inflammatory disease usually caused by bacteria. Progression is rapid and very difficult to treat. A disability exists when there is impairment of renal function, due to any chronic kidney disease with chronic hemodialysis or peritoneal dialysis necessitated by irreversible renal failure; or kidney transplant. Consider under a disability for 12 months following surgery; thereafter, evaluate residual impairment; or persistent elevation of serum creatinine to 4 mg per 100 cc or greater or reduction of creatinine clearance to 20 ml per minute (29 liters per 24 hours) or less, over at least 3 months with one of the following: 1. Renal osteodystrophy manifested by severe bone pain and appropriate x-ray abnormalities (osteitis fibrosa, severe osteoporosis, pathologic fractures); or 2. A clinical episode of pericarditis; or 3. Persistent motor or sensory neuropathy; or 4. Persistent itching; or 5. Persistent fluid overload syndrome resulting in diastolic hypertension (110 mm or above) or signs of vascular congestion; or 6. Persistent anorexia with recent weight loss and current weight meeting the Social Security Administration values; or 7. Persistent hematocrits of 30% or less.

Rectal Prolapse - the herniation of some or all of the layers of the rectum through the anus. Surgery is the definitive treatment. Recurrence varies from a few to 1/3 of all patients. The principal complication following surgery is anal incontinence. Anal incontinence can be corrected with a colostomy, which is no cause for disability.

Regional Enteritis (also known as Granulomatous ileitis; ileocolitis; Crohn's disease) - a degenerative, chronic, intermittent, inflammatory disease which can affect any part of the gastrointestinal system, but most commonly affects the terminal ileum (the lower portion of the small intestine which is about 12 ft. in length). There is chronic diarrhea, abdominal pain, fever, anorexia, weight loss, intestinal stenosis, distention, vomiting, or chronic disability from malnutrition, and painful fistulas and abscesses may form. There is cause for disability when regional enteritis is demonstrated by operative findings, barium studies, biopsy, or endoscopy with persistent or recurrent intestinal obstruction evidenced by abdominal pain, distention, nausea, and vomiting and accompanied by stenotic areas of small bowel with proximal intestinal dilation; or persistent or recurrent systemic manifestations such as arthritis, iritis, fever, or liver dysfunction, not attributable to other causes; or intermittent obstruction due to intractable abscess or fistula formation; or extreme weight loss as described by the Social Security Administration.

Renal Failure (Acute) - ischemic or toxic, reversible loss of normal kidney function. The mortality is high even with appropriate therapy. If there is glomerular destruction, death is almost certain. See Pyelonephritis for disability criteria for renal impairment.

Renal Failure (Chronic) - the ability of the kidneys to excrete urine is gradually impaired. This condition is terminal unless there is a successful kidney transplant. See Pyelonephritis for disability criteria for chronic kidney disease.

Renal Function Impairment - impairment or reduction of the ability of the kidneys to extract wastes from the blood and excrete it as urine. It is due to injury, surgery or chronic kidney diseases such as hypertensive vascular disease, chronic nephritis, nephrolithiasis, etc. Usually hemodialysis, peritoneal dialysis or eventually a kidney transplant is necessary. Criteria for disability is listed in detail under Pyelonephritis (Chronic).

Restrictive Pericarditis (Chronic) - a condition in which firm scar tissue forms or there is a gradual accumulation of fluid which fills the pericardial cavity thus preventing normal filling of the ventricles. It is also known as chronic constrictive pericarditis. This condition is usually secondary to such diseases as chronic kidney failure, radiation therapy, cancer, TB, pyogenic, viral or histoplasmosis infection. The only early symptom is diastolic hypertension. Later manifestations are shortness of breath, inability to breathe unless sitting or standing, cough, rales, engorgement of the neck veins, pleural effusion, hepatomegaly, ascites and edema of hands and legs. Surgical decortication (removal of scar tissue) is the treatment of choice with 80% of all cases having good results. If a disability exists, it would be treated the same as CHF, hypertensive vascular disease or ischemic heart disease.

Retinitis Pigmentosa - a hereditary disease in which there is atrophy of the retina, pigment deposits, loss of rods and cones, and cataract formation. Prognosis depends upon the amount of involvement around the optic nerve. If there is a great deal of involvement, progressive blindness occurs. Disability would depend upon the degree of impairment, but most cases are covered by total bilateral blindness.

Retinitis Proliferans - an eye disorder that is the result of recurrent hemorrhage from the retina into the vitreous. It is connective tissue containing blood vessels which project into the vitreous thus impairing vision. This condition is the major cause of blindness and is frequent in diabetics. Control of the diabetes and blood pressure are important in slowing the progression of retinitis proliferans. A new procedure utilizing a laser beam is very successful in slowing the progression of this condition. Disability depends upon the extent of impairment of central visual acuity or peripheral visual fields or loss of visual efficiency.

Rotator Cuff Syndrome - a condition that may be a simple inflammation or a tear of the musculotendinous cuff of the shoulder seen mostly in the middle aged or the elderly. The patient may experience pain and weakness or may not be able to lift the arm. The period and degree of disability varies according to the severity of the condition. A severe tear requires surgery while most cases of inflammation respond to rest, heat, massage, anti-inflammatory drugs and exercise. Care must be taken to prevent recurrence because this is a painful chronic condition. Disability falls under the criteria for disability for soft tissue injuries of an upper extremity. This requires a series of staged surgical procedures within 12 months after onset for salvage and/ or restoration of major function of the extremity, such major function not being restored or not expected to be restored within 12 months after onset.

Sarcoma of Soft Parts - cancer of tissue other than bone or cartilage. This is cause for disability when the sarcoma is not controlled by prescribed therapy.

Schizophrenia - the most common type of psychosis, characterized by changes in behavior, mood and perception. It usually begins in early adult life. The subtypes are: A. Hebephrenic schizophrenia-a condition characterized by hypochondria, thought disorganization, inappropriate and unpredictable reactions and various mannerisms. B. Catatonic schizophrenia--extreme withdrawal, refusal to speak, stiff posture and may be impulsive or dangerous. C. Paranoid schizophrenia-- extreme suspicion of people and things. Delusions and hallucinations are common. All of these patients are unpredictable and pose a threat of injury to themselves or others. Hospitalization, sedation, ECT, and psychotherapy are a must, with emphasis on returning the patient to a normal life. These patients are usually able to maintain an adequate to marginal level of behavior for variable lengths of time. Recurring breakdowns are the usual and the possibility of homicide or suicide is always present. See Psychosis for disability criteria.

Scleroderma or Progressive Systemic Sclerosis (PSS) (Scleroderma is the skin also.) - A chronic disease of unknown origin, characterized by fibrosis and vascular abnormalities in the skin, joints and internal organs. The disease may be mild with a normal life span, or so severe as to cause death due to CHF, chronic kidney disease, pulmonary manifestations or intestinal malabsorption. The most common complaints at first are spasms of blood vessels in the fingers followed by cyanosis and swelling in the joints. Other symptoms are generalized joint pain, muscle weakness, intestinal disturbances, symmetrical hardening of the skin on the fingers and arms, the skin becomes shiny and tight with increased discoloration, the face becomes mask-like, with discolorations appearing on the fingers, lips and tongue. Also, pulmonary hypertension develops, a form of biliary cirrhosis develops, tendinitis, ulcers on the fingers, esophageal dysfunction (the most frequent visceral disturbance, eventually occurring in most patients), distention, restrictive and obstructive ventilary disease, pleurisy, pericarditis, pleural effusion, cardiac arrhythmias, conduction disturbances, CHF or chronic renal failure develop. The criteria for disability is sceleroderma or progressive systemic sclerosis (the diffuse or generalized form), with advanced limitation in the use of the hands due to sclerodactylia (hardening of the fingers) or limitation in other joints; or significant visceral manifestations of digestive, cardiac, pulmonary or renal impairment.

Scoliosis - an abnormal side-to-side curvature of the spine. Whether or not a disability exists is dependent upon the degree of impairment of locomotion or respiratory function.

Senile Dementia and Alzheimer's Disease - 1. Senile dementia-a process of intellectual deterioration which may affect all people over 65. Memory of recent events and judgment are usually affected first. 2. Alzheimer's disease-the same as senile dementia except that it occurs before age 65 and in the absence of any demonstrable cause. These patients usually become helpless long before death. Death is due to another cause. Both senile dementia and Alzheimer's dementia are considered for disability under Chronic Brain Syndrome when accompanied by both A and B: A. Demonstrated deterioration in intellectual functioning, manifested by persistence in one or more of the following clinical signs: 1. Marked memory defect for recent events; or 2. Impoverished, slowed, perseverative thinking, with confusion or disorientation; or 3. Labile, shallow, or coarse affect. B. Resulting persistence of marked restriction of daily activities and constriction of interests and deterioration in personal habits and seriously impaired ability to relate to other people.

Sickle Cell Disease - a form of anemia that affects black people and is characterized by sickle-shaped red blood cells. This condition is inherited as a recessive trait. Other names are: sickle cell anemia, Hb S disease, drepanocytic anemia and meniscocytosis. Symptoms of this disease are severe anemia, jaundice, arthralgia with fever, recurrent ulcers about the ankles, episodes of severe abdominal pain and vomiting, partial paralysis and other neurological disturbances, thrombosis and infarction. There is cause for disability for sickle cell disease (or one of its variants) when it is accompanied by documented painful (thrombotic) crises occurring at least 3 times during the 5 months prior to adjudication; or when it requires extended hospitalization (beyond emergency care) at least 3 times during the 12 months prior to adjudication. The resulting impairment under the criteria for the affected body systems should also be evaluated.

Sigmoid Volvulus - an obstruction of the sigmoid colon. Circulatory impairment may accompany the obstruction causing gangrene. (Congenital megacolon and Chagas' disease may predispose). This disease is seen mostly in the elderly or in those with severe psychiatric or neurological disorders. Surgery is the definitive treatment. It may require a simple resection or a colostomy. Sigmoid volvulus and colostomy are not in themselves cause for disability.

Spondylolisthesis and Spondylolysis - these conditions are peculiar to the 5th lumbar vertebra. Spondylolisthesis refers to the subluxation of the 5th lumbar vertebra (L5).

Spondylolysis is a condition ofL5 in which the cartilaginous disc of the vertebra breaks down either unilaterally or bilaterally. The result of both conditions is unilateral (usually) compression of a nerve root which causes pain, partial paralysis, numbness, loss of reflex, wasting of muscles, and sometimes urine retention or anal incontinence. In most cases, 2 weeks of conservative treatment with bed rest (supine and on a firm surface), pain relievers and mild tranquilizers is sufficient. When there is urine retention and/ or anal incontinence or cases that are persistent after prescribed treatment, surgery is indicated. For the cause for disability of spondylolisthesis see herniated nucleus pulposus. The criteria for disability of spondylolysis is x-ray evidence of either a compression fracture of a vertebral body with loss of at least 50% of the estimated height of the vertebral body prior to the compression fracture, with no intervening direct traumatic episode; or multiple fractures of vertebrae with no intervening direct traumatic episode.

Sprained Back - torn supraspinous ligament. This condition is suggested when the onset is sudden after heavy lifting or other strenuous physical exertion. There is pain and tenderness localized over the area affected. This condition responds well to treatment and is not cause for a disability.

Status Anginosus - a chronic condition of angina pectoris caused by a blood supply restricted due to hardening and narrowing of arteries supplying the heart muscle. The characteristics of angina are usually constant for any individual, any change in the pattern should be considered a serious change. See Chest Pain of Cardiac Origin for criteria for disability.

Suppurative (Acne) - acne with pus-filled cysts. It may be cause for disability when accompanied by extensive lesions involving the axillae or perineum not responding to prescribed treatment and not amenable to surgical treatment.

Thromboangiitis Obliterans (Buerger's Disease) - an inflammation of the inner lining of small and medium-sized arteries and veins (less frequently in veins) of the extremities in a segmental pattern. There is a definite relationship between heavy smoking and the occurrence and progression of the disease. The onset may be gradual or sudden with rapid development of gangrene. Some symptoms are coldness, numbness, tingling, burning, intermittent claudication, pain when the disease is severe, pallor when leg or arm is elevated, red when standing or in use; there may be ulcers and thrombophlebitis. There is a disability when accompanied by arteriosclerosis obliterans or thromboangitis with intermittent claudication (arterial spasm with cramping in the leg followed by lameness) with failure to visualize (on arteriogram) the common femoral or deep femoral artery in one extremity; or intermittent claudication and absence of peripheral arterial pulsations in the femoral, popliteal, dorsalis pedis, and posterior tibial arteries by doppler or plethysmography, in one extremity; or amputation at or above the tarsal region due to peripheral vascular disease.

Thrombocytopenia - a deficiency disease that is a result of the decrease in number of thrombocytes (platelets) in the blood. For various reasons there is failure of production, increased destruction, increased utilization or dilution of the blood platelets. Symptoms are an increased tendency to bleed, demonstrated by bleeding into the skin and mucosa, bleeding in the gastrointestinal tract and genito-urinary system. Chronic thrombocytopenia (due to any cause) is cause for disability when the platelet count is repeatedly below 40,000/ cubic millimeter, with at least one spontaneous hemorrhage, requiring transfusion, Within 5 months prior to adjudication; or intracranial bleeding within 12 months prior to adjudication.

Tinnitus - "ringing" in the ears. In itself tinnitus is not cause for disability unless it becomes persistent and is associated with a disturbance in balance or a loss of hearing.

Transmural Myocardial Infarction - an infarction (death of tissue) that involves the whole thickness of the myocardium from the epicardium to the endocardium and is characterized by abnormal Q waves on EKG. See Myocardial Infarction for symptoms and disability.

Tuberculosis (TB) - an acute or chronic infection caused by the bacilli, Mycobacterium tuberculosis or Mycobacterium bovis (rare in the U.S.). TB usually affects the lungs, but may spread via the blood or lymph to any part of the body. The disease is most commonly spread through the air. In the early stages, there are no symptoms. Later, lesions will show on x-ray, fever, fatigue, weight loss, hemoptysis, pleural or chest pain, and dyspnea will develop. Complications of TB are respiratory failure, pulmonary hypertension or cor pulmonale. The treatment usually consists of 2 antituberculosis drugs for 2 years. The prognosis where there is lung involvement alone is good. When it is more widespread, the prognosis depends upon the extent of the disease. Types of TB other than pulmonary are: 1. Extrapulmonary tuberculosis-spreads by the blood or lymph or by sputum to the upper air passages, mouth and GI tract. Extrapulmonary TB is generally easier to treat because the environments are not as favorable for bacteria growth as the lungs. Treatment follows the same general regimen as pulmonary TB-2 antituberculosis agents for 2 years. 2. Miliary tuberculosis (also called generalized hematogenous or lymphohematogenous tuberculosis)-this type of tuberculosis is spread by the blood and lymph and usually causes tuberculin metastasis in the blood or bone. Chest x-rays and tuberculin tests may be negative. There is high fever, toxemia, and tuberculous meningitis is a common complication. When the bone marrow is involved, there is anemia, thrombocytopenia and possibly leukemia. There is good response to treatment. 3. Central nervous system tuberculosis or tuberculous meningitis-develops when the tubercle bacilli get into the cerebrospinal fluid. There is significant alteration of consciousness from drowsiness to coma. There may be permanent complications such as convulsive disorders, hydrocephalus, mental retardation and neurological impairments. (Usual TB treatment.) 4. Pleural tuberculosis- TB in the pleura caused by pleural effusion and tuberculous empyema (pus in the pleura). A very common complication is bronchopleural fistula which must be drained surgically. 5. Tuberculous pericarditis-pericarditis caused by the TB bacterium. This causes constrictive pericarditis and may leave chronic constrictive pericarditis. This infection usually responds to TB therapy, but since it is difficult to diagnose, there may be permanent damage. 6. Genito-urinary TB-spread by the bloodstream. Response to therapy is usually prompt. 7. Tuberculosis of the GI tract-TB of the small and large intestines are the most common. Responds well to tuberculin chemotherapy. 8. TB of bones and joints-

a. TB of peripheral joints (usually affects 1 joint at a time) produces a purulent arthritis which responds well to TB therapy. b. Tuberculous spondylitis (Pott's disease)-a serious form of TB which affects the spine frequently causing neurological damage. Compression of the spinal cord by a paraspinal abscess or granular tissue causes symptoms ranging from minor loss of sphincter control to sudden and irreversible paralysis. Posterior spinal fusion is the treatment of choice, along with TB chemotherapy. 9. Other types are: a. TB of the adrenals-causes Addison's disease. b. Tuberculous peritonitis-responds well to treatment. c. Tuberculous lymphadenitis-responds well to treatment. d. Tuberculosis of the mouth, middle ear, larynx, and bronchial tree-response of all of these to TB therapy is prompt and permanent. The criteria for disability evaluation of pulmonary tuberculosis that is caused by Mycobacterium tuberculosis where there is impairment of pulmonary function due to extensive disease should be evaluated under the criteria for chronic obstructive airway disease or diffuse pulmonary fibrosis or other restrictive ventilary disorders. Tuberculous-meningitis-induced convulsive disorders, mental retardation, and neurological impairments would have to be evaluated under each respective impairment. Chronic (tuberculous) constrictive pericarditis, joint impairment due to peripheral joint TB, and paralysis due to Pott's disease would have to be evaluated by the criteria for each system involved.

Tumors of the Back - neoplasms classified as both primary and metastatic, benign and malignant are divided into 2 groups: 1. Extramedullary neoplasms-those occurring outside of the spinal column and which affect the bony vertebrae and their associated structures. The first symptoms occur as the result of compression of nerve roots-pain, partial paralysis, sensory loss, and muscular weakness. Sphincter control may be affected and there may be blockage of spinal vessels. These tumors can usually be removed by surgery, but the prognosis depends on the damage already done. 2. Intramedullary neoplasms (gliomas and ependymomas)- those tumors which are inside the spinal column. The symptoms usually begin with loss of sensation turning to pain in the fingers, then there is a loss of sensation across the back and shoulders, the legs may become weak and spastic, vertigo, facial sensory impairment, speech impairment and early loss of sphincter control may develop. Intramedullary tumors are inoperable except for decompression procedures. Radiotherapy is helpful in some cases. These tumors can only be arrested and recurrence is sure. There is disability for spinal cord or nerve root lesions due to any cause with disorganization of motor function.

Ulcerative Colitis - a chronic inflammation of the colon which results in ulcers, fibrosis and shortening of the entire colon. Hemorrhage, toxic megacolon and cancer are complications of prolonged or recurrent attacks. Toxic megacolon should be treated as a medical emergency or death may result. The criteria for disability is chronic ulcerative or granulomatous colitis which must be demonstrated by endoscopy, barium enema, biopsy or operative findings with: recurrent bloody stools documented on repeated examinations and anemia manifested by hematocrit of 30% or less on repeated examinations; or persistent or recurrent manifestations (systemic), such as arthritis, iritis, fever, or liver dysfunction, not attributable to other causes; or intermittent obstruction due to intractable (hard to cure) abscesses, fistula formation, or stenosis; or recurrence of the above after total colectomy; or extreme weight loss {according to the Social Security Administration values).

Unstable Angina {also called acute coronary insufficiency, pre-infarction angina or the intermediate syndrome) - Unstable angina is so named because the status of the patient is unstable. Very frequently, unstable angina leads to an acute myocardial infarction. For disability see Chest Pain of Cardiac Origin and Myocardial Infarction (more detailed).

Uterine Leiomyomas or Fibromyomas - as known as fibroid tumors)-these tumors are benign and are the most common tumor of the female reproductive system. The definitive treatment is a hysterectomy with an excellent prognosis. This condition is not cause for disability except in rare cases wherein the fibroids become malignant.

Vaginal Malignancy - cancer in the vagina. Primary malignant tumors arising in the vagina are rare, but metastasis from cancer of the cervix, bladder and rectum are common. Neither treatment by surgery nor radiation nor chemotherapy is considered satisfactory. Fewer than 1/3 survive 5 years after the diagnosis. In addition, surgical treatment is difficult for the patient to accept because the rectum, bladder and all reproductive organs must be removed. There is cause for disability under the classification of recurrent malignancy with metastasis under either urinary bladder, uterus, or rectum, etc.

Vagotomy - surgical cutting of the vagus nerve to relieve severe pain usually associated with a gastrectomy or other painful GI condition. A vagotomy in itself does not constitute a cause for disability.

Variant Angina {also called Prinzmetal's angina) - angina characterized by attacks that occur at night while the patient is resting or sleeping, and by unusual changes in E KG readings; usually due to spasms of the coronary arteries. For the criteria for disability see Chest Pain of Cardiac Origin and Myocardial Infarction.

Ventricular Aneurysm - a ballooning-out of the wall of one of the ventricles of the heart due to weakening of the wall by disease, injury, or abnormality at birth. They usually develop after a transmural myocardial infarction, they do not rupture, they cause ventricular arrhythmias, they show a persistent elevation of S-T segments on EKG and they are a threat as a source of thrombi or emboli. Surgical repair is the definitive treatment when the patient can stand it. If it cannot be repaired, the patient has the symptoms of congestive heart failure. This condition would be evaluated for disability under Myocardial Infarction since it is the primary disease involved.

Ventricular Fibrillation or Asystole - the ventricles stop contracting effectively and begin a circus-like movement. The patient will lose consciousness immediately, arterial pulse and respiration will be absent, blood pressure will be negligible, the pupils become dilated and the skin turns blue. Treatment must be immediate because there is irreversible damage to the heart and brain within 2-4 minutes. CPR, electric; shock, and epinephrine are indicated. Therapy must be maintained until normal respirations and heart action return or until the patient is pronounced dead. If the patient survives, there is definitely a disability. It may be under Congestive Heart Failure, or Recurrent Arrhythmias.

Ventricular Tachycardia - the ventricles contract at a high rate of 150-250 beats per minute independently of the atria. It may be caused by myocardial ischemia, infarction, ventricular aneurysm or digitalis or quinidine intoxication. Prognosis depends upon whether or not ventricular fibrillation develops. Ventricular tachycardia would be classified for disability under ischemic heart disease, myocardial infarction or recurrent arrhythmia (not due to digitalis).

Vertigo - a sensation of dizziness and/or whirling. The prognosis depends upon the underlying cause. There is cause for disability if the vertigo is accompanied by frequent attacks of balance disturbance, tinnitus and a progressive loss of hearing.

Vestibular Disorder (Labyrinthine Vestibular Disturbance) - disturbance of one's equilibrium usually as a result of a disease of or injury to the vestibular branch of the 8th cranial nerve. There is cause for disability when there is a disturbance of the labyrinthine vestibular function characterized by a history of frequent attacks of balance disturbance, tinnitus, and a progressive loss of hearing with both A and B: A. Disturbed function of vestibular labyrinth demonstrated by caloric or other vestibular tests; and B. Hearing loss established by audiometry.

Visual Efficiency (Loss of) - the visual efficiency of one eye is the product of the percentage of central vision efficiency and the percentage of visual field efficiency. There is a disability when the visual efficiency of the better eye after best correction is 20% or less.

ABOUT THE AUTHORS

JERROLD ZIVIC, J.D.

Jerry is a recently-retired attorney and has had a successful national Social Security Disability Practice where he helped thousands of individuals get their Social Security Disability Benefits. He is now a media commentator where he shares his unique perspective and passion for helping others.

Full Bio:

Jerry was the founder of a national Social Security Disability law practice who helped individuals get the benefits they earned from the government for over 30 years.
He currently, as a retired attorney, uses his education and passion for helping others. You can find him regularly as a television commentator and radio guest on topics of social security disability, social security retirement, veteran's issues, ADA and special needs individuals.

He has authored articles and has lectured at various organizations and for multiple associations. He taught a course to attorneys about social security disability. He has supported many charities and served on many boards, including the Certification of Disability Management Specialists Commission where he was a Public Commissioner and served as Chairman of the Professional Conduct Committee. He hosted a National Social Security Disability conference for long term disability insurance companies for 8 years. He also has been a member of a number of attorney-related organizations.

In his free time, he enjoys spending time with his family, going to movies, golfing with friends, and trying to find the time to catch an occasional sporting event. His friends can attest to his dry wit and his ability to think outside of the box and find solutions for problems that nobody else can.

AARON ZIVIC, J.D., M.P.A.

Aaron has been around Social Security Disability all of his life and spent many hours working at his father's law firm. This allowed him the opportunity to learn the nuances of social security law. Following in his father's footsteps, Aaron attended law school and is now an attorney concentrating in healthcare law. Aaron resides in Chicago with his wife Aliza.

Full Bio:

Aaron was born and raised in the Chicago area. He received a Bachelor of Arts (BA) from Washington University in St. Louis where he majored in Political Science and minored in General Business. After college, Aaron participated in a fellowship abroad in the Middle East. As part of the fellowship, Aaron worked at a nonprofit organization specializing in microcredit loans to local entrepreneurs. That year stoked Aaron's interest in politics and naturally led him to Washington DC. There, Aaron took courses at the Georgetown Public Policy Institute (GPPI).

Although Aaron enjoyed his time in the nation's capital, he felt something missing in his life and returned home to his roots in Chicago to be with family and friends. As a young adult, Aaron was influenced by the time he spent working at his father's Social Security Disability Law practice. Through this experience, Aaron gained an appreciation for the law and how it could help the sick and disabled. Aaron decided to pursue law and attended Chicago-Kent College of Law where he earned a Juris Doctor (JD). During his time in law school, Aaron spent two semesters working in the school's Health and Disability Law Clinic. In addition, he earned The Center for Computer Assisted Legal Instruction (CALI) Award for the highest grade in his Negotiations course.

Concurrently, Aaron obtained a Master's in Public Administration (MPA) from the University of Illinois-Chicago where he secured a merit scholarship. Law and public policy are intertwined and gaining knowledge in both disciplines offers Aaron a more complete perspective on social issues.

Currently, Aaron is a healthcare attorney and concentrates in Medicaid issues. He co-authored an article with his father Jerry Zivic entitled "Views on Social Security: Baby Boomers vs. Generation Y" which Appeared in Today's Senior Magazine.

Aaron is an avid sports fan and supports all Chicago sports teams, despite all of the "suffering" that entails. Aaron resides in Chicago with his wife Aliza.

BOOKS BY THE AUTHORS

How To Keep Your Social Security Benefits: Tips, Tools and Strategies for Success (Volume 1)

How To Keep Your Social Security Benefits: Tips, Tools and Strategies for Success (Volume 2) --- Coming Soon!

How To Keep Your Social Security Benefits: Tips, Tools and Strategies for Success (Volume 3) --- Coming Soon!

www.ingramcontent.com/pod-product-compliance
Lightning Source LLC
Chambersburg PA
CBHW052309220526
45472CB00001B/46